Table of Contents

Introduction ....
    Who is this Book Aimed For? 4
    Version Used 5
    Practice Worksheets 5
    How this Book is Structured 5
    Comments 6

Chapter 1: What is XLOOKUP? 7
    XLOOKUP Syntax 7
    XLOOKUP Arguments 8

Chapter 2: XLOOKUP vs VLOOKUP 10
    What is VLOOKUP? 10
    Limitations of VLOOKUP 12

Chapter 3: Relative & Absolute Cell References 16
    Relative Cell References 16
    Absolute Cell References 18
    Naming a Cell 21

Chapter 4: Performing Vertical Lookups Using XLOOKUP 24

Chapter 5: Performing Horizontal Lookups Using XLOOKUP 32

Chapter 6: How to Handle Errors with XLOOKUP 37
    Types of Errors in Excel 37
    How to use the If_Not_Found Argument 38
    Additional Notes 41

Chapter 7: How to Perform an Approximate Match with XLOOKUP 42
    Sorting the Data Table 46
    Handling Errors in an Approximate Match 47

Chapter 8: Perform Partial Matches with XLOOKUP 4
Excel Wildcard Characters 4
How to do a Partial Match with XLOOKUP 4
Chapter 9: How to Extract the Last Value with XLOOKUP 5
The Search_Mode Argument 5
Extracting the Last Value 5
Chapter 10: Extracting Multiple Values with XLOOKUP 5
What is Spilled? 5
Chapter 11: How to Perform Two-Way Lookups 6
Additional Resources 6
More Books by Excel Master Consultant 6
Leave a Review 7

Copyright © 2020
Copyright Protection

All rights reserved. No part of this publication may be reproduced, distributed, or transmitted in any form or by any means, including photocopying, recording, or other electronic or mechanical methods, without the prior written permission of the publisher, except in the case of brief quotations embodied in critical reviews and certain other non-commercial uses permitted by copyright law.

Your Free Bonus Gift!

As a small token of thanks for buying this book I would like to offer a **FREE** bonus gift to all my readers. I am offering a **FREE** online VBA macros course called ***How to Record Macros in Excel***.

In this **FREE** course you will learn:

- How to record a macro to eliminate manual repetitive Excel tasks
- How to execute a macro by:
    - Using the Macro Dialog Box
    - Using the Visual Basic Editor
    - Clicking a button
    - Clicking a shape

Once you have completed the course you will be able to:

- Automate Excel tasks easily
- Save valuable time
- Advance your Excel skills

You can register for this **FREE** online VBA course by entering the below link to your web browser.

https://mailchi.mp/8b8d27df975c/how-to-record-macros-in-excel

Introduction

Over the years, Excel has improved and new features and tools have been introduced to make it even better. One such new feature is the XLOOKUP function. Microsoft have created this new function because they have listened to people who have used VLOOKUP and HLOOKUP on a regular basis and expressed their frustration at some of the limitations they possess. These limitations will be explained in chapter 2 of the book. Microsoft have taken these points on board and created their best and most flexible lookup function yet!

Who is this Book Aimed For?

This book is aimed for people who:

- Have a basic understanding of Excel, know how to open and save workbooks, enter data in worksheets and have a general familiarity with the Excel ribbon and its tools. If you are an absolute beginner then you would be better off starting with my Excel beginner's book called **Excel Bible for Beginners: The Essential Step by Step Guide to Learn Excel for Beginners**. You can purchase this book from Amazon by entering the below link to your web browser:

  https://www.amazon.com/Excel-Bible-Beginners-Essential-Guide/dp/B088JS6YVS

- Know how to create simple formulas in a worksheet

- Have used lookup functions before such as VLOOKUP, HLOOKUP, LOOKUP, INDEX+MATCH and would now like to learn how to use XLOOKUP to perform more efficient lookups

- Work with large amounts of data and need to extract certain information from it quickly and easily

- Want to take their Excel skills to the next level

- Would like to save time and become more efficient using their spreadsheets

Version Used

At the time of writing, XLOOKUP is only available in Office 365 so all the examples shown in this book are used in this Office package. For you to use XLOOKUP and follow along, you must have Office 365.

Practice Worksheets

Before starting this book, I recommend that you download the free practice worksheets. These worksheets are available to anybody who has purchased this book. Each tab in the workbook is named after a chapter number so you know which worksheet to use for each chapter. Following along in each chapter will reinforce what you have learnt and it helps absorb the information better. You can download the free worksheets by entering the below link to your web browser and then entering your details so that I can send them to your email address.

https://bit.ly/2O64tAO

How this Book is Structured

I will be using the same data set called **Employee Database** throughout the book to perform the various lookups in each chapter. If you have downloaded the practice worksheets then this will be in the **Employee Database (Vertical)** tab for vertical lookups and **Employee Database (Horizontal)** tab for horizontal lookups. In chapter 11, where I will be talking you through how to do two-way lookups, I will be using a different data set which is in the **Chapter 11 Worksheet** tab in your practice worksheets.

This book will build your knowledge of XLOOKUP as you go through chapter by chapter. At the beginning of the book, I will talk you through what XLOOKUP is and then discuss why it is better and more flexible than VLOOKUP. I will then talk about relative and absolute cell references because when you create XLOOKUP formulas you often copy them down columns or across rows. Knowing the difference between the two cell reference types is important because if done incorrectly, Excel will return incorrect results or errors.

In the middle and latter sections of the book, you will get your hands dirty and be able to try XLOOKUP for yourself. I will show you lots of examples of how to create XLOOKUP formulas such as vertical and horizontal lookups, doing an approximate match, extracting the last value in a column, and doing partial lookups using wildcard characters. I will also show you how to handle errors if XLOOKUP returns an error and also teach you how to create more complex XLOOKUP formulas such as two-way lookups by nesting an XLOOKUP function inside another.

Comments

I hope you enjoy reading this book as much as I have enjoyed writing it and that it enables you to take your Excel skills to the next level. Learning this excellent function will not only make you more efficient and save you time, it could also help get you a pay rise as you will find new ways to streamline your work and ultimately help the business you work for.

I am always interested to hear from my readers and I am very grateful for any comments and reviews I receive for my books. Please do leave me a review on Amazon and you can also leave a comment on my website www.excelmasterconsultant.com.

Now please read on to start your XLOOKUP journey.

Chapter 1: What is XLOOKUP?

The XLOOKUP function is the successor to other Excel lookup functions such as VLOOKUP, HLOOKUP, LOOKUP and the INDEX+MATCH functions. It was released in 2020 and is only currently available in Office 365 at the time of writing. So why have Microsoft released another lookup function when there is already VLOOKUP, and HLOOKUP available? Well, the main reason is that these functions have their limitations which I will discuss in the next chapter. XLOOKUP is far more versatile and eliminates the need to use VLOOKUP and HLOOKUP as it does everything these functions can do and more.

So, what does XLOOKUP do? The XLOOKUP function allows you to search for an item and return a value from a column or row in a data set. For example, you can search for a student in a data set and retrieve what grade he/she has achieved or search for a product in a product table and retrieve its price. If XLOOKUP doesn't find an exact match you can return the closest match. You will learn more about this in chapter 7. As you read each chapter, I will show you many examples of how XLOOKUP works and why you should use it instead of VLOOKUP or HLOOKUP if you have Office 365. But first, I will show you what the XLOOKUP syntax is and then explain its arguments.

XLOOKUP Syntax

As with any Excel function, you must start with an equals sign (=). The syntax of XLOOKUP is as follows:

=XLOOKUP (lookup_value, lookup_array, return_array, [if_not_found], [match_mode], [search_mode])

XLOOKUP Arguments

As you can see, XLOOKUP has 6 arguments, 3 are mandatory and 3 are optional. The arguments in brackets are the optional arguments. I will briefly explain what each argument is but as you go further in the book you will see how they work when I give you various examples of XLOOKUP in action.

1) **lookup_value** – The value you are looking for in the column or row of the data set

2) **lookup_array** – The column or row of the data set to search the lookup value

3) **return_array** – The value you want to return from the column or row of the data set

4) **[if_not_found]** – This is an optional argument. The value to return if the lookup value is not found. If you do not specify this argument then Excel will return a #N/A error

5) **[match_mode]** – This is an optional argument. With this argument you can specify the type of match you want by selecting one of the following options:

   - **0 - Exact match**
     The lookup value should exactly match the value in the lookup array. This is the default option

   - **-1 - Exact match or next smaller item**
     This looks for an exact match but if the exact match is not found then it looks for the next smallest value

   - **1 - Exact match or next larger item**
     This looks for an exact match but if the exact match is not found then it looks for the next largest value

- **2 - Wildcard character match**
  This is to perform partial matching by using wildcard characters such as an asterisk (*), question mark (?) or a tilde (~)

6) **[search_mode]** – This is an optional argument. If this argument is selected, you can specify how XLOOKUP performs its search of the lookup array. You can select one of four options:

- **1 - Search first-to-last**
  XLOOKUP will search for the lookup value in the lookup array from top to bottom. This is the default option

- **-1 - Search last-to-first**
  XLOOKUP will search for the lookup value in the lookup array from bottom to top. This is useful if you want to find the last value

- **2 - Binary search (sorted ascending order)**
  This performs a binary search. The data needs to be sorted in ascending order first otherwise XLOOKUP can return an error or a wrong result

- **-2 - Binary search (sorted descending order)**
  This performs a binary search. The data needs to be sorted in descending order first otherwise XLOOKUP can return an error or a wrong result

To summarise, XLOOKUP can search for values in horizontal and vertical ranges, basically eliminating the need to use VLOOKUP and HLOOKUP. As you can see from its arguments, you do not need to use the IFERROR function to handle #NA errors. It can also handle approximate and exact matches as well as support wildcard characters to search for partial matches. You can even return the last value from a column instead of just the first value. You can now start to see the benefits of using XLOOKUP instead of VLOOKUP and HLOOKUP and begin to realise how flexible this Excel function is.

Chapter 2: XLOOKUP vs VLOOKUP

XLOOKUP is the number one lookup function to use in Excel because of its ease and flexibility over other lookup functions. This is why it is important to learn how to use it as soon as you can if you use Excel on a regular basis and you have Office 365. VLOOKUP comes with many limitations which I will describe in this chapter. Some of the limitations can be overcome with work arounds like combining VLOOKUP with other Excel functions but this can be time consuming to construct and even more difficult to read. XLOOKUP will eliminate all this hassle and save you time in the process.

What is VLOOKUP?

Before I talk about the limitations of VLOOKUP, I must stress that VLOOKUP is one of the most popular and widely used Excel functions available. So what does VLOOKUP do? It essentially looks for a value in a column in a data set and returns a value from another column in the same row. For example, you may have a worksheet that contains information about employees such as their employee ID number, first name, last name, date of birth and job title. You can search for an employee ID number and return the details of the employee based on the column number you specify in the col_index_num argument. XLOOKUP can do this too but much more!

Its syntax is:

=VLOOKUP(lookup_value, table_array, column_index, [match_mode])

1) **lookup_value** – The value you are looking for in the left most column of the table

2) **table_array** – The table from which you want to retrieve the value

3) **col_index_num** – The column number in the table array in which you want to retrieve the value

4) **[range_lookup]** –This is an optional argument. If you select FALSE then it is an exact match. If you select TRUE then it is an approximate match. The default setting is TRUE

To explain this further, I will use the below example to show you how VLOOKUP works.

	A	B	C	D	E	F	G
1	Employee ID	First Name	Last Name	Job Title		Employee ID	102
2	100	Sarah	Blake	Sales Rep		Job Title	IT Manager
3	101	Jim	Smith	Marketing Manager			
4	102	James	Dowsett	IT Manager			
5	103	Lisa	Manning	HR Manager			
6	104	Hardeep	Singh	Finance Controller			
7							

G2 =VLOOKUP(G1,A1:D6,4,FALSE)

Here we have a table which contains information about each employee in the range A1:D6 which lists all the employee ID numbers, their first and last names, and their job titles. I want to extract the job title for employee ID number 102 which is in cell G1 and enter it in cell G2.

The VLOOKUP formula in cell G2 is:

=VLOOKUP(G1,A1:D6,4,FALSE)

I will break this formula down by each of its arguments to explain how this works:

lookup_value – This is the employee ID number in cell G1

table_array – This is the data set in the range A1:D6

col_index_num – The job title is in column 4 of the range A1:D6 so enter 4 in this argument

range_lookup – I want to return an exact match, so I enter FALSE i the argument

If you are new to VLOOKUP then understanding how this works will b key to understanding XLOOKUP when I go through various example later in the book.

Limitations of VLOOKUP

So, what I described above sounds great and performs a complex role wel So what is actually wrong with the VLOOKUP function? Here I will lis some of the issues with VLOOKUP.

VLOOKUP is Slow

VLOOKUP is very slow as it requires you to reference an entire data set You won't notice much difference if you have a data set with a few hundre rows. The problem occurs when you have a data set which contain hundreds of thousands of rows. Excel will take a while to recalculate whicl is frustrating and time consuming. With XLOOKUP, you reference les cells as it only requires you to reference the relevant rows or columns. A XLOOKUP references less cells the calculation times are much quicke than VLOOKUP.

Default Setting is an Approximate Match

The fourth argument (range_lookup) is an optional argument i VLOOKUP but it is set to an approximate match. Most people who us VLOOKUP want to do an exact match so they will have to specify FALSI in this argument. If you omit this argument but would like to do an exac match then VLOOKUP may give you an error or an incorrect result. This means that in theory, even though this argument is optional you will still have to specify FALSE each time you want an exact match. Microsoft have fixed this issue with XLOOKUP because the default setting for the match_mode argument is an exact match.

VLOOKUP only Looks to the Right

VLOOKUP only looks to the right of the lookup value. In the VLOOKUP example above, if the employee ID number was in the last column then it would not work. XLOOKUP can look to the left or to the right of the lookup value which means you don't have to manipulate the data set for it to work.

VLOOKUP can't do Horizontal Lookups

VLOOKUP stands for vertical lookup. This means it can look vertically but not horizontally. You would have to use HLOOKUP for this. XLOOKUP can look vertically and horizontally which eliminates the need to use VLOOKUP and HLOOKUP.

Column Numbers are Hard Coded

In the col_index_num argument of VLOOKUP you have to enter a column number. For example, if you want to return a value in the third column then you have to type in 3. However, what happens if you insert a new column in the data set? The col_index_num argument will still be 3 but VLOOKUP will return the value from the wrong column. With XLOOKUP you can insert as many new columns as you like and it will not break the formula as you don't need to specify a column index number.

VLOOKUP only Finds the First Value

With VLOOKUP you can only extract the first value as it searches from the top row in a column to the bottom. With XLOOKUP, the search_mode argument allows you to specify how you want XLOOKUP to search for a value. If you want to extract the last value then XLOOKUP can start its search from the bottom row of a column and work its way upwards.

VLOOKUP can't Perform Binary Searches

With VLOOKUP you can't do binary searches but with XLOOKUP you can.

You Have to Sort Data for an Approximate Match

In order to perform an approximate match in VLOOKUP you have to sort the table from smallest to largest first otherwise it will give an incorrect result or an error. With XLOOKUP you can perform an approximate match without sorting the table first which saves you time and hassle. I will demonstrate this in chapter 7.

VLOOKUP can't Return an Approximate Match Value that is Higher

When you do an approximate match with VLOOKUP you can't return a value that is higher. You can however do this with XLOOKUP as well as returning a value that is lower. I will demonstrate this in chapter 7.

VLOOKUP can't Handle Errors

Whenever the lookup value is not found in the data table in VLOOKUP it will return a #N/A error. In order to handle these errors you would have to wrap the VLOOKUP formula with an IFERROR, IFNA or ISNA function. This makes your formula more complex and difficult to read. With XLOOKUP there is an argument where you can elegantly handle #N/A errors using the if_not_found argument. This will be explained in more detail in chapter 6.

For further reading on this subject, I have also written a blog on the limitations of VLOOKUP on my website which you can read by entering the link below in your web browser:

https://www.excelmasterconsultant.com/single-post/2018/10/19/Limitations-of-VLOOKUP-Five-Big-Limitations-of-the-VLOOKUP-Function

Below is a table which summarises what I have mentioned above. You can now see the benefits of using XLOOKUP over VLOOKUP.

XLOOKUP vs VLOOKUP	XLOOKUP	VLOOKUP
Fast Calculation Speed	✓	X
Default Exact Match	✓	X
Looks to the Right	✓	✓
Looks to the Left	✓	X
Horizontal Lookup	✓	X
Insert new Columns	✓	X
Search First Value	✓	✓
Search Last Value	✓	X
Binary Search	✓	X
Don't Need to Sort Data for Approximate Match	✓	X
Return Approximate Match with Lower Value	✓	✓
Return Approximate Match with Higher Value	✓	X
Handle Errors without using Other Functions	✓	X

Chapter 3: Relative & Absolute Cell References

This chapter will explain what relative and absolute cell references are. You need to understand the difference between the two when you are copying formulas down a column or across rows otherwise the formulas will return errors or incorrect results. Understanding the difference between the two can take you from being an Excel novice to a master in no time.

Relative Cell References

A relative cell reference is the default behaviour of a formula. Relative cell references change when the formula is copied to another cell in the worksheet.

In the above example, there is a simple formula in cell C1 which adds the values in cell A1 and B1 together. The formula is **=A1+B1**.

Now, when I copy the formula to cell G1, it is relative to cell G1 so the formula becomes =**E1+F1**.

Let us take a look at another example.

	A	B	C	D	E
	AVERAGE ▼ : ✗ ✓ f_x			=B2*C2	
	A	B	C	D	E
1	Product	Unit Price	Qty	Sales	
2	Bananas	$1.99	15	=B2*C2	
3	Apples	$1.50	12		
4	Oranges	$2.00	19		
5	Pears	$1.99	17		
6	Grapes	$2.50	10		
7					

In the above example, I want to work out the sales for each fruit by multiplying the unit price by the quantity. The formula in cell D2 is =**B2*C2**. I use relative cell references because I want to copy the formula down to cell D6 so it will calculate the sales for each fruit in the other rows. To copy the formula down use the fill handle which is located in the bottom right corner of the cell you want to copy.

	A	B	C	D	E
D2	▼ : ✗ ✓ f_x	=B2*C2			
	A	B	C	D	E
1	Product	Unit Price	Qty	Sales	
2	Bananas	1.99	15	=B2*C2	
3	Apples	1.5	12	=B3*C3	
4	Oranges	2	19	=B4*C4	
5	Pears	1.99	17	=B5*C5	
6	Grapes	2.5	10	=B6*C6	
7					

When I copy the formula down to cell D6, you can see how the formula references each row, i.e. the row number changes in the formula as you copy it down.

Absolute Cell References

There may be occasions when you do not want the cell reference to change when you are copying formulas. With absolute cell references you keep the row and column constant. You specify whether a cell will be absolute by placing a dollar sign ($) before the column and row. If the dollar sign ($) is before the column or the row and not both then it is called a mixed cell reference.

$A$1	The column and the row stay constant when copied
A$1	The row stays constant but the column changes when copied
$A1	The column stays constant but the row changes when copied

The table above shows you how to make a cell reference absolute or mixed.

When you want to enter the dollar sign ($) to make the cell reference absolute or mixed, you can click in the cell and press the F4 key. This is much quicker than if you were to enter the dollar sign ($) manually.

You can keep on pressing the F4 key to toggle between where the dollar signs ($) will be placed. When you press the F4 key once it places the dollar signs ($) before the column and the row to make the cell reference absolute. When you press F4 again it places the dollar sign ($) before the row only. When you press the F4 key the third time it places the dollar sign before the column only. Finally, when you press the F4 key the fourth time it does not place any dollar signs ($), making the cell reference relative.

Let us look at a simple example of an absolute cell reference to start with.

Cell A1 contains the number 6 and the formula in cell C1 is =**$A$1**

Now, when I copy the formula and paste it to another area of the worksheet such as cell D6, the formula is still referencing cell A1. This is because the column and row is constant as it has a dollar sign ($) before the column and row.

I will now show you another example of an absolute cell reference.

	A	B	C	D	E	F	G
1	Sales Rep	Sales	Bonus		Bonus	10%	
2	Jim	$10,000	=B2*$F$1				
3	Sarah	$5,000					
4	Lynn	$12,000					
5	James	$7,500					
6	Wasim	$6,000					
7							

In the above example, I want to apply a 10% bonus to each Sales Rep based on their sales. The formula in cell C2 is =**B2*$F$1**. Notice that cell F1 is an absolute cell reference because I want to keep on referencing cell F1 when I copy the formula down the rows. Also notice that cell B2 is a relative cell reference because I want to reference each row number when I copy the formula down.

	A	B	C	D
1	Sales Rep	Sales	Bonus	
2	Jim	10000	=B2*$F$1	
3	Sarah	5000	=B3*$F$1	
4	Lynn	12000	=B4*$F$1	
5	James	7500	=B5*$F$1	
6	Wasim	6000	=B6*$F$1	
7				

When the formula is copied down, notice that the absolute cell reference i.e. cell F1 is constant but the cells in column B are relative i.e. the row number changes when the formula is copied down.

What happens if I don't make cell F1 absolute?

	A	B	C	D	E	F	G
	AVERAGE		fx =B3*F2				
1	Sales Rep	Sales	Bonus		Bonus	10%	
2	Jim	$10,000	$1,000				
3	Sarah	$5,000	=B3*F2				
4	Lynn	$12,000					
5	James	$7,500					
6	Wasim	$6,000					
7							

Well, when I copy the formula down to cell C3, notice that F1 becomes F2 and the formula multiplies the sales with a blank cell. If the formula is copied down to cell C4 then it would multiply the sales by cell F3 and so on.

Naming a Cell

Another way to make a cell absolute is to name the cell. The main advantage of naming a cell is that it makes the formula easier to read. I will explain the steps on how to name a cell by using the same example as in the absolute cell reference section where I apply a 10% bonus to each Sales Rep. I would like to name the 10% bonus in cell F1 "Bonus". Here is how to do this:

1) Select cell F1 and in the **Name Box** which is located to the left of the Formula Bar type "**Bonus**" and then press **Enter**

	A	B	C	D	E	F	G
	Bonus		fx 10%				
1	Sales Rep	Sales	Bonus		Bonus	10%	
2	Jim	$10,000					
3	Sarah	$5,000					
4	Lynn	$12,000					
5	James	$7,500					
6	Wasim	$6,000					
7							

21

2) Now, instead of entering the formula =B2*$F$1 enter =**B2*Bonus**

	A	B	C	D	E	F	G
		B2		fx	=B2*Bonus		
1	Sales Rep	Sales	Bonus		Bonus	10%	
2	Jim	$10,000	=B2*Bonus				
3	Sarah	$5,000					
4	Lynn	$12,000					
5	James	$7,500					
6	Wasim	$6,000					
7							

3) Copy the formula down to cell C6

	A	B	C	D	E	F	G
1	Sales Rep	Sales	Bonus		Bonus	10%	
2	Jim	$10,000	$1,000				
3	Sarah	$5,000	$500				
4	Lynn	$12,000	$1,200				
5	James	$7,500	$750				
6	Wasim	$6,000	$600				
7							

4) Notice the named cell called "Bonus" remains constant

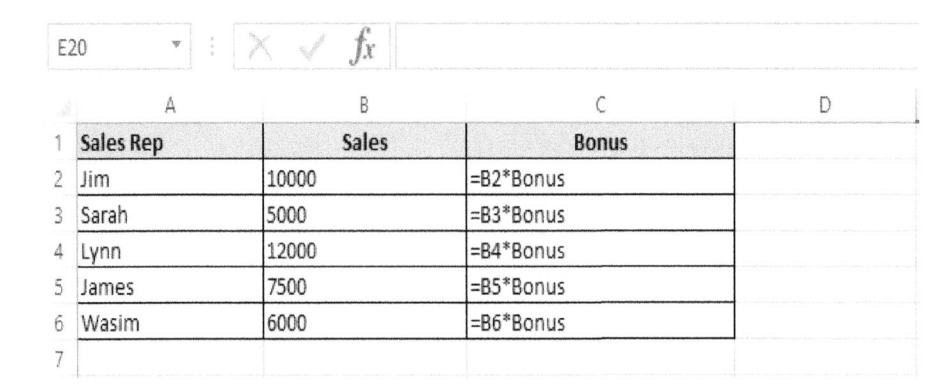

E20

	A	B	C	D
1	Sales Rep	Sales	Bonus	
2	Jim	10000	=B2*Bonus	
3	Sarah	5000	=B3*Bonus	
4	Lynn	12000	=B4*Bonus	
5	James	7500	=B5*Bonus	
6	Wasim	6000	=B6*Bonus	
7				

Understanding relative and absolute cell references is very important when you are performing XLOOKUP formulas as you will be referencing columns, rows or both and then copying formulas down or across. Knowing the difference between the two and understanding how they behave when cells are copied and filled to other cells will mean you will not get incorrect results and errors.

Chapter 4: Performing Vertical Lookups Using XLOOKUP

Now that you know what XLOOKUP is, what the syntax and its arguments are and you know the difference between relative and absolute cell references, I will now show you various examples of how to use XLOOKUP. In this chapter, I will first show you the most basic function of XLOOKUP which is how to perform vertical lookups. This will perform the same function as VLOOKUP but as mentioned in chapter 2, XLOOKUP is much faster as it does not reference the whole data table as you will soon find out.

Practice Worksheets

If you would like to follow along then please use the **Employee Database (Vertical)** tab and the **Chapter 4 Worksheet** tab in your practice worksheets

	A	B	C	D	E	F	G	H
1	Employee ID	Date Started	Address	Name	Years in Service		Years in Service	Loyalty Bonus
2	1011	04/09/2011	67 Tapping Close	Jim Faraday	8		2	$100
3	1015	19/02/2005	12 Brow Hill Way	Hardeep Kang	14		5	$200
4	1029	12/08/2016	19 Little Field Street	Raul Gonzalez	3		10	$400
5	1089	11/07/2014	90 Thomas Road	Liz Smith	5		15	$600
6	1105	28/04/2001	67 Pasture Street	Emma Jane	18		20	$800
7	1146	08/05/1998	145 Beacroft Avenue	Sara Kenny	21		25	$1,000
8	1178	14/04/2007	289 Price Street	Jessica Campbell	12			
9	1297	06/11/1992	128 Byron Avenue	Mick Taylor	27			
10	1356	27/12/1997	45 Wordsworth Street	Rosie Jenkins	22			
11	1398	24/01/2018	266 Long Hall Street	Michael Kane	1			
12	1404	04/10/2019	405 Milton Street	Jason Peters	0			
13	1478	14/02/2011	19 Foxes Way	Veronica Bridge	8			
14	1499	09/10/2009	99 Leyfield Cross	James Porter	10			
15	1556	18/09/2006	44 Shelley Avenue	Simon James	13			
16	1089	11/07/2014	87 Narrow Hall Way	Liz Smith	5			
17	1599	27/11/2017	72 Crossfield Street	William Gamble	2			
18	1626	21/04/2019	189 Burns Avenue	Michelle Conner	0			
19	1688	16/02/2015	52 Golds Way	Tess Kelly	4			
20	1727	09/05/2016	456 Hampton Way	Jenny Fuller	3			
21	1799	14/06/1991	288 Strand Street	Angie Greene	28			

The above screenshot is an employee database which shows all the employees who work for a company. The database contains the names of the employees, their ID numbers, the date they started working at the company, where they live and how many years they have been working at the company. This employee database is located in the **Employee Database (Vertical)** tab in your practice worksheets.

	A	B	C	D	E
1	Name	Date Started	Address	Years in Service	
2	Angie Greene				
3	Emma Jane				
4	Hardeep Kang				
5	James Porter				
6	Jason Peters				
7	Jenny Fuller				
8	Jessica Campbell				
9	Jim Faraday				
10	Liz Smith				
11	Liz Smith				
12	Michael Kane				
13	Michelle Conner				
14	Mick Taylor				
15	Raul Gonzalez				
16	Rosie Jenkins				
17	Sara Kenny				
18	Simon James				
19	Tess Kelly				
20	Veronica Bridge				
21	William Gamble				

The goal is to populate the above spreadsheet and fill in the date they started in column B, their address in column C and the number of years they have been working at the company in column D using the information from the employee database in the **Employee Database (Vertical)** tab. This spreadsheet is located in the **Chapter 4 Worksheet** tab in your practice worksheets.

Populating the Date Started

First, I will populate the date each employee started in column B.

	A	B	C	D
1	Name	Date Started	Address	Years in Service
2	Angie Greene	14/06/1991		
3	Emma Jane			
4	Hardeep Kang			
5	James Porter			
6	Jason Peters			
7	Jenny Fuller			
8	Jessica Campbell			
9	Jim Faraday			
10	Liz Smith			
11	Liz Smith			
12	Michael Kane			
13	Michelle Conner			
14	Mick Taylor			
15	Raul Gonzalez			
16	Rosie Jenkins			
17	Sara Kenny			
18	Simon James			
19	Tess Kelly			
20	Veronica Bridge			
21	William Gamble			

B2 cell formula: =XLOOKUP(A2,'Employee Database (Vertical)'!$D$2:$D$21,'Employee Database (Vertical)'!$B$2:$B$21)

The formula in cell B2 is:

=XLOOKUP(A2,'Employee Database (Vertical)'!$D$2:$D$21,'Employee Database (Vertical)'!$B$2:$B$21)

I will break this formula down by its arguments to explain how this works:

lookup_value – The lookup value is the name of the employee in cell A2 in the **Chapter 4 Worksheet** tab

lookup_array – The lookup array are the names of the employees in the **Employee Database (Vertical)** tab. This is the range D2:D21. Notice the range is an absolute cell reference as I will be copying the XLOOKUP formula down to cell B21 in the **Chapter 4 Worksheet** tab

return_array – The return array are the dates I want to return from the **Employee Database (Vertical)** tab. This is the range B2:B21. Notice the range is an absolute cell reference as I will be copying the XLOOKUP formula down to cell B21 in the **Chapter 4 Worksheet** tab

The if_not_found, match_mode and search_mode arguments are optional, and I do not need these, so I closed the bracket after the return_array argument.

	A	B	C	D	E
1	Name	Date Started	Address	Years in Service	
2	Angie Greene	14/06/1991			
3	Emma Jane	28/04/2001			
4	Hardeep Kang	19/02/2005			
5	James Porter	09/10/2009			
6	Jason Peters	04/10/2019			
7	Jenny Fuller	09/05/2016			
8	Jessica Campbell	14/04/2007			
9	Jim Faraday	04/09/2011			
10	Liz Smith	11/07/2014			
11	Liz Smith	11/07/2014			
12	Michael Kane	24/01/2018			
13	Michelle Conner	21/04/2019			
14	Mick Taylor	06/11/1992			
15	Raul Gonzalez	12/08/2016			
16	Rosie Jenkins	27/12/1997			
17	Sara Kenny	08/05/1998			
18	Simon James	18/09/2006			
19	Tess Kelly	16/02/2015			
20	Veronica Bridge	14/02/2011			
21	William Gamble	27/11/2017			

You can then copy the formula down to cell B21 to return the dates each employee started at the company. Remember, because I made the range in the lookup_array and return_array arguments absolute cell references, when I copied the formula down it returns the correct results.

Note:

In a VLOOKUP formula, I would not be able to perform this task because the lookup value, i.e. the column with the employee names is to the right of the value I want to return, i.e. the date started column in the employee database. Remember, VLOOKUP only looks from left to right so for this to work, the column with the employee names would have to be moved to the very first column in the employee database. The great benefit of XLOOKUP is that you do not have to manipulate the data first to perform lookups.

Populating the Address of the Employees

To populate the employees address in column C in the **Chapter Worksheet** tab, you follow the same process as when you extract the date started.

	A	B	C	D
1	Name	Date Started	Address	Years in Service
2	Angie Greene	14/06/1991	288 Strand Street	
3	Emma Jane	28/04/2001		
4	Hardeep Kang	19/02/2005		
5	James Porter	09/10/2009		
6	Jason Peters	04/10/2019		
7	Jenny Fuller	09/05/2016		
8	Jessica Campbell	14/04/2007		
9	Jim Faraday	04/09/2011		
10	Liz Smith	11/07/2014		
11	Liz Smith	11/07/2014		
12	Michael Kane	24/01/2018		
13	Michelle Conner	21/04/2019		
14	Mick Taylor	06/11/1992		
15	Raul Gonzalez	12/08/2016		
16	Rosie Jenkins	27/12/1997		
17	Sara Kenny	08/05/1998		
18	Simon James	18/09/2006		
19	Tess Kelly	16/02/2015		
20	Veronica Bridge	14/02/2011		
21	William Gamble	27/11/2017		

Formula in C2: =XLOOKUP(A2,'Employee Database (Vertical)'!$D$2:$D$21,'Employee Database (Vertical)'!$C$2:$C$21)

The formula in cell C2 is:

=XLOOKUP(A2,'Employee Database (Vertical)'!$D$2:$D$21,'Employee Database (Vertical)'!$C$2:$C$21)

The lookup_value and the lookup_array arguments remains the same because you are still looking up the employee name in the **Chapter 4 Worksheet** tab and searching for it in the column containing the employee names in the **Employee Database (Vertical)** tab. The only difference is the return_array argument. For this, I want to return the address of each employee and the addresses are in the range C2:C21 in the **Employee Database (Vertical)** tab.

	A	B	C	D
1	Name	Date Started	Address	Years in Service
2	Angie Greene	14/06/1991	288 Strand Street	
3	Emma Jane	28/04/2001	67 Pasture Street	
4	Hardeep Kang	19/02/2005	12 Brow Hill Way	
5	James Porter	09/10/2009	99 Leyfield Cross	
6	Jason Peters	04/10/2019	405 Milton Street	
7	Jenny Fuller	09/05/2016	456 Hampton Way	
8	Jessica Campbell	14/04/2007	289 Price Street	
9	Jim Faraday	04/09/2011	67 Tapping Close	
10	Liz Smith	11/07/2014	90 Thomas Road	
11	Liz Smith	11/07/2014	90 Thomas Road	
12	Michael Kane	24/01/2018	266 Long Hall Street	
13	Michelle Conner	21/04/2019	189 Burns Avenue	
14	Mick Taylor	06/11/1992	128 Byron Avenue	
15	Raul Gonzalez	12/08/2016	19 Little Field Street	
16	Rosie Jenkins	27/12/1997	45 Wordsworth Street	
17	Sara Kenny	08/05/1998	145 Beacroft Avenue	
18	Simon James	18/09/2006	44 Shelley Avenue	
19	Tess Kelly	16/02/2015	52 Golds Way	
20	Veronica Bridge	14/02/2011	19 Foxes Way	
21	William Gamble	27/11/2017	72 Crossfield Street	

You can then copy the formula down to cell C21 in the **Chapter 4 Worksheet** tab.

Populating the Years in Service

Finally, I can populate how long each employee has worked at the company.

| D2 | | × | ✓ | fx | =XLOOKUP(A2,'Employee Database (Vertical)'!$D$2:$D$21,'Employee Database (Vertical)'!$E$2:$E$21 |

	A	B	C	D
1	Name	Date Started	Address	Years in Service
2	Angie Greene	14/06/1991	288 Strand Street	28
3	Emma Jane	28/04/2001	67 Pasture Street	
4	Hardeep Kang	19/02/2005	12 Brow Hill Way	
5	James Porter	09/10/2009	99 Leyfield Cross	
6	Jason Peters	04/10/2019	405 Milton Street	
7	Jenny Fuller	09/05/2016	456 Hampton Way	
8	Jessica Campbell	14/04/2007	289 Price Street	
9	Jim Faraday	04/09/2011	67 Tapping Close	
10	Liz Smith	11/07/2014	90 Thomas Road	
11	Liz Smith	11/07/2014	90 Thomas Road	
12	Michael Kane	24/01/2018	266 Long Hall Street	
13	Michelle Conner	21/04/2019	189 Burns Avenue	
14	Mick Taylor	06/11/1992	128 Byron Avenue	
15	Raul Gonzalez	12/08/2016	19 Little Field Street	
16	Rosie Jenkins	27/12/1997	45 Wordsworth Street	
17	Sara Kenny	08/05/1998	145 Beacroft Avenue	
18	Simon James	18/09/2006	44 Shelley Avenue	
19	Tess Kelly	16/02/2015	52 Golds Way	
20	Veronica Bridge	14/02/2011	19 Foxes Way	
21	William Gamble	27/11/2017	72 Crossfield Street	

The formula in cell D2 in the **Chapter 4 Worksheet** tab is:

=XLOOKUP(A2,'Employee Database (Vertical)'!$D$2:$D$21,'Employee Database (Vertical)'!$E$2:$E$21)

Again, the lookup_value and the lookup_array arguments remains the same. The only difference is the return_array argument. For this, I want to return the years in service of each employee, and this is in the range E2:E21 in the **Employee Database (Vertical)** tab.

	A	B	C	D
1	Name	Date Started	Address	Years in Service
2	Angie Greene	14/06/1991	288 Strand Street	28
3	Emma Jane	28/04/2001	67 Pasture Street	18
4	Hardeep Kang	19/02/2005	12 Brow Hill Way	14
5	James Porter	09/10/2009	99 Leyfield Cross	10
6	Jason Peters	04/10/2019	405 Milton Street	0
7	Jenny Fuller	09/05/2016	456 Hampton Way	3
8	Jessica Campbell	14/04/2007	289 Price Street	12
9	Jim Faraday	04/09/2011	67 Tapping Close	8
10	Liz Smith	11/07/2014	90 Thomas Road	5
11	Liz Smith	11/07/2014	90 Thomas Road	5
12	Michael Kane	24/01/2018	266 Long Hall Street	1
13	Michelle Conner	21/04/2019	189 Burns Avenue	0
14	Mick Taylor	06/11/1992	128 Byron Avenue	27
15	Raul Gonzalez	12/08/2016	19 Little Field Street	3
16	Rosie Jenkins	27/12/1997	45 Wordsworth Street	22
17	Sara Kenny	08/05/1998	145 Beacroft Avenue	21
18	Simon James	18/09/2006	44 Shelley Avenue	13
19	Tess Kelly	16/02/2015	52 Golds Way	4
20	Veronica Bridge	14/02/2011	19 Foxes Way	8
21	William Gamble	27/11/2017	72 Crossfield Street	2

I can now copy the formula down to cell D21.

Note:

Notice that the lookup value, i.e. the column containing the employee names are to the left of the return array, i.e. the column that contains the number of years in service in the **Employee Database (Vertical)** tab. You can therefore perform this lookup in a VLOOKUP formula without having to manipulate the data set first.

In this chapter I have performed lookups where I have extracted values to the left and to the right of the return array which shows the flexibility of XLOOKUP.

Chapter 5: Performing Horizontal Lookups Using XLOOKUP

In the previous chapter, I showed you how to perform vertical lookups, i.e. looking up values vertically in a column. Sometimes you may have data where you cannot perform vertical lookups because it is arranged horizontally. Before XLOOKUP you would have to use HLOOKUP, but you can now also perform lookups horizontally using XLOOKUP.

> **Practice Worksheets**
>
> If you would like to follow along then please use the **Employee Database (Horizontal)** tab and the **Chapter 5 Worksheet** tab in your practice worksheets

	A	B	C	D	E	F	G	H	I	J
1	Employee ID	1011	1015	1029	1089	1105	1146	1178	1297	1356
2	Date Started	04/09/2011	19/02/2005	12/08/2016	11/07/2014	28/04/2001	08/05/1998	14/04/2007	06/11/1992	27/12/1997
3	Address	67 Tapping Close	12 Brow Hill Way	19 Little Field Street	90 Thomas Road	67 Pasture Street	145 Beacroft Avenue	289 Price Street	128 Byron Avenue	45 Wordsworth Stree
4	Name	Jim Faraday	Hardeep Kang	Raul Gonzalez	Liz Smith	Emma Jane	Sara Kenny	Jessica Campbell	Mick Taylor	Rosie Jenkins
5	Years in Service	8	14	3	5	18	21	12	27	22
6										

The above screenshot is the same employee database but instead of it being displayed vertically in columns it is displayed horizontally in rows. This is in the **Employee Database (Horizontal)** tab in your practice worksheets.

	A	B	C
1	Employee ID	1089	
2	Address		
3	Date Started		
4	Name		
5	Years in Service		
6			

The goal is to populate the address, the date started, name and years in service for employee ID number 1089. To follow along, please use the **Chapter 5 Worksheet** tab.

Populating the Address

First, I will populate the address for employee number 1089.

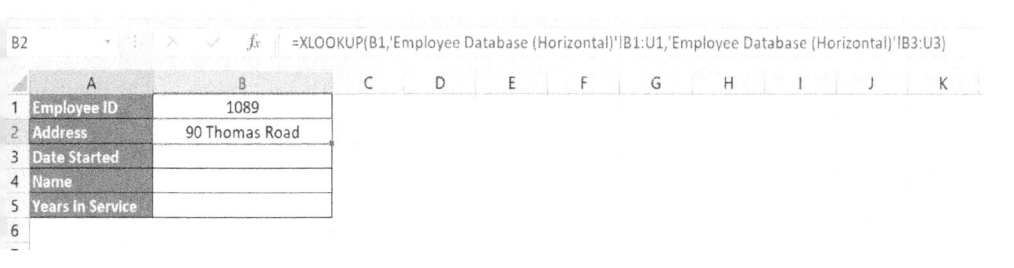

	A	B
1	Employee ID	1089
2	Address	90 Thomas Road
3	Date Started	
4	Name	
5	Years in Service	
6		

B2 formula: =XLOOKUP(B1,'Employee Database (Horizontal)'!B1:U1,'Employee Database (Horizontal)'!B3:U3)

The formula in cell B2 is:

=XLOOKUP(B1,'Employee Database (Horizontal)'!B1:U1,'Employee Database (Horizontal)'!B3:U3)

To explain how this formula works, I will break it down by its arguments:

lookup_value – The lookup value is the employee ID number in cell B1 in the **Chapter 5 Worksheet** tab

33

lookup_array – The lookup array is the employee ID numbers in the **Employee Database (Horizontal)** tab. This is the range B1:U1. Notice that the range is a relative cell reference as I will not be copying the XLOOKUP formula down. You can also make this an absolute cell reference if you wish

return_array – The return array is the address I want to return from the **Employee Database (Horizontal)** tab. This is the range B3:U3. Again, I have made this a relative cell reference as I will not be copying the XLOOKUP formula down, but you can also make this an absolute cell reference if you want

The if_not_found, match_mode and search_mode arguments are optional, and I do not need these, so I closed the bracket after the return_array argument.

Populating the Date Started

The next step is to enter the start date for employee ID 1089.

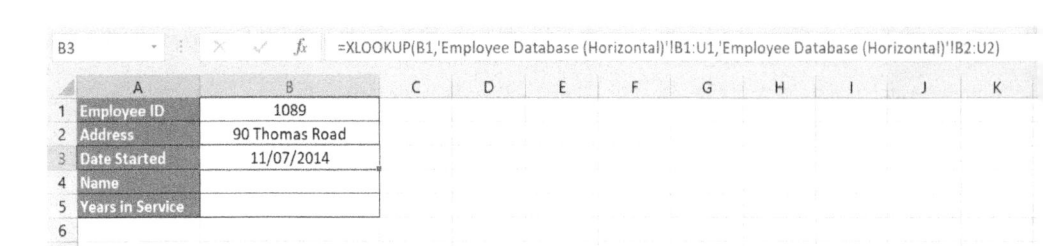

	A	B
1	Employee ID	1089
2	Address	90 Thomas Road
3	Date Started	11/07/2014
4	Name	
5	Years in Service	
6		

B3 formula: =XLOOKUP(B1,'Employee Database (Horizontal)'!B1:U1,'Employee Database (Horizontal)'!B2:U2)

The formula in cell B3 is:

=XLOOKUP(B1,'Employee Database (Horizontal)'!B1:U1,'Employee Database (Horizontal)'!B2:U2)

The only difference between this formula and the previous one is the return_array argument. The date started dates are in row 2 of the

Employee Database (Horizontal)** tab so therefore the return_array argument is B2:U2.

Populating the Employee Name

I will now lookup the employee name for employee ID 1089.

B4   fx   =XLOOKUP(B1,'Employee Database (Horizontal)'!B1:U1,'Employee Database (Horizontal)'!B4:U4)

	A	B
1	Employee ID	1089
2	Address	90 Thomas Road
3	Date Started	11/07/2014
4	Name	Liz Smith
5	Years in Service	

The formula to extract the employee name in cell B4 is:

=XLOOKUP(B1,'Employee Database (Horizontal)'!B1:U1,'Employee Database (Horizontal)'!B4:U4)

The employee names are in row 4 in the **Employee Database (Horizontal)** tab so therefore the return_array argument is B4:U4. The lookup_value and the lookup_array arguments remain the same as the previous two XLOOKUP formulas.

Populating the Years in Service

Finally, I will populate the number of years in service for employee ID 1089 in the **Chapter 5 Worksheet** tab.

B5   fx   =XLOOKUP(B1,'Employee Database (Horizontal)'!B1:U1,'Employee Database (Horizontal)'!B5:U5)

	A	B
1	Employee ID	1089
2	Address	90 Thomas Road
3	Date Started	11/07/2014
4	Name	Liz Smith
5	Years in Service	5

The formula in cell B5 is:

=XLOOKUP(B1,'Employee Database (Horizontal)'!B1:U1,'Employee Database (Horizontal)'!B5:U5)

The years in service is in row 5 of the **Employee Database (Horizontal)** tab so the return_array argument is B5:U5.

The great thing about XLOOKUP is that if the data table is re-arranged XLOOKUP will still give the correct results.

	A	B	C	D	E	F	G	H	I	J
1	Date Started	04/09/2011	19/02/2005	12/08/2016	11/07/2014	28/04/2001	08/05/1998	14/04/2007	06/11/1992	27/12/1997
2	Address	67 Tapping Close	12 Brow Hill Way	19 Little Field Street	90 Thomas Road	67 Pasture Street	145 Beacroft Avenue	289 Price Street	128 Byron Avenue	45 Wordsworth St
3	Name	Jim Faraday	Hardeep Kang	Raul Gonzalez	Liz Smith	Emma Jane	Sara Kenny	Jessica Campbell	Mick Taylor	Rosie Jenkins
4	Employee ID	1011	1015	1029	1089	1105	1146	1178	1297	1356
5	Years in Service	8	14	3	5	18	21	12	27	22

For example, the above screenshot shows the lookup array, i.e. the employee ID row, has changed from row 1 to row 4.

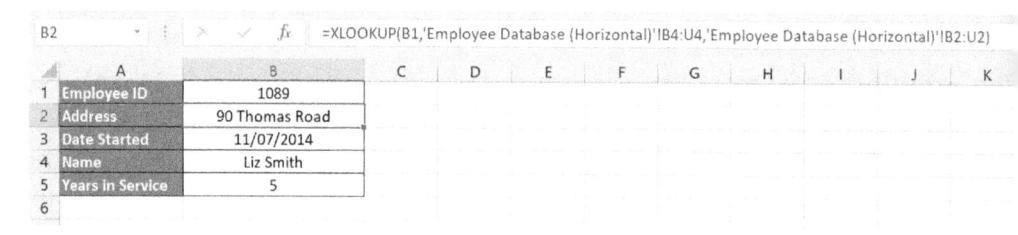

B2   fx =XLOOKUP(B1,'Employee Database (Horizontal)'!B4:U4,'Employee Database (Horizontal)'!B2:U2)

	A	B
1	Employee ID	1089
2	Address	90 Thomas Road
3	Date Started	11/07/2014
4	Name	Liz Smith
5	Years in Service	5

However, the results have remained the same. Notice the lookup_array argument has changed from B1:U1 to B4:U4 to take into account the employee ID has moved from row 1 to row 4.

Note:

With HLOOKUP, if the employee ID is in row 4 in the employee database and you try and extract the date started, address and the name of the employee then it will return a #N/A error. This is because the lookup array needs to be in the very first row of the data table. HLOOKUP can only look from top to bottom and not bottom to top just like VLOOKUP can only look from left to right and not right to left. Again, this shows the flexibility of XLOOKUP compared to VLOOKUP and HLOOKUP.

Chapter 6: How to Handle Errors with XLOOKUP

As with other lookup functions, if the lookup value is not found in the data table then XLOOKUP will return an error. With VLOOKUP, HLOOKUP, LOOKUP and INDEX+MATCH functions you have to wrap the formula with an error handling function such as an IFERROR or IFNA. This can make your formula longer and therefore harder to read if you ever need to go back and edit it. With XLOOKUP, there is an optional argument to handle any errors called the if_not_found argument. If Excel returns a #N/A error for example, you can return something more meaningful instead such as "No Data Found". This makes your spreadsheet cleaner and more professional.

Types of Errors in Excel

Before I explain how to use the if_not_found argument, I will explain the different errors that may occur when using XLOOKUP.

#N/A Error

Arguably, the most common error that occurs when you write lookup formulas is the #N/A error. This means the lookup value is not found in the column or array. It could be that an approximate match must be used. I will explain how to do an approximate match in chapter 7.

#VALUE Error

The #VALUE error can occur if the lookup and return arrays have incompatible dimensions. For example, searching in a horizontal array and returning values from a vertical array or vice versa.

#REF Error

If one of the columns or rows in the data set was deleted and XLOOKUP was referencing one of these columns or rows in the lookup_array or return_array argument then Excel will return a #REF error.

#DIV/0! Error

If you are looking up numbers using XLOOKUP and performing calculations with these numbers, but it is dividing by either a 0 or an empty cell then Excel will return a #DIV/0! error.

#NUM! Error

If your data set contains numbers but it is manually fixed with a currency symbol such as a $ or a percentage sign (%) and then you try and perform calculations with these numbers you will get the #NUM! error. When you fix a number with a currency symbol or a % then the number becomes a text.

#NAME? Error

The #NAME? can occur if Excel does not recognise something in the formula or function. The most common reason for this error is when you have misspelled the function name or a named range. You can also get this error if you haven't entered any quotation marks on any text in the formula.

How to use the If_Not_Found Argument

I will now explain how the if_not_found argument works in XLOOKUP.

Practice Worksheets

If you would like to follow along then please use the **Employee Database (Vertical)** tab and the **Chapter 6 Worksheet** tab in your practice worksheets

	A	B	C	D	E
1	Employee ID	Date Started	Address	Name	Years in Service
2	1011	04/09/2011	67 Tapping Close	Jim Faraday	8
3	1015	19/02/2005	12 Brow Hill Way	Hardeep Kang	14
4	1029	12/08/2016	19 Little Field Street	Raul Gonzalez	3
5	1089	11/07/2014	90 Thomas Road	Liz Smith	5
6	1105	28/04/2001	67 Pasture Street	Emma Jane	18
7	1146	08/05/1998	145 Beacroft Avenue	Sara Kenny	21
8	1178	14/04/2007	289 Price Street	Jessica Campbell	12
9	1297	06/11/1992	128 Byron Avenue	Mick Taylor	27
10	1356	27/12/1997	45 Wordsworth Street	Rosie Jenkins	22
11	1398	24/01/2018	266 Long Hall Street	Michael Kane	1
12	1404	04/10/2019	405 Milton Street	Jason Peters	0
13	1478	14/02/2011	19 Foxes Way	Veronica Bridge	8
14	1499	09/10/2009	99 Leyfield Cross	James Porter	10
15	1556	18/09/2006	44 Shelley Avenue	Simon James	13
16	1089	11/07/2014	87 Narrow Hall Way	Liz Smith	5
17	1599	27/11/2017	72 Crossfield Street	William Gamble	2
18	1626	21/04/2019	189 Burns Avenue	Michelle Conner	0
19	1688	16/02/2015	52 Golds Way	Tess Kelly	4
20	1727	09/05/2016	456 Hampton Way	Jenny Fuller	3
21	1799	14/06/1991	288 Strand Street	Angie Greene	28
22					

I will be using the employee database in the **Employee Database (Vertical)** tab.

	A	B	C	D
1	Name	Date Started	Address	Years in Service
2	Dan James			
3				

I want to enter the date started, address and the years in service for Dan James in cells B2, C2 and D2. This is in the **Chapter 6 Worksheet** tab in your practice worksheets.

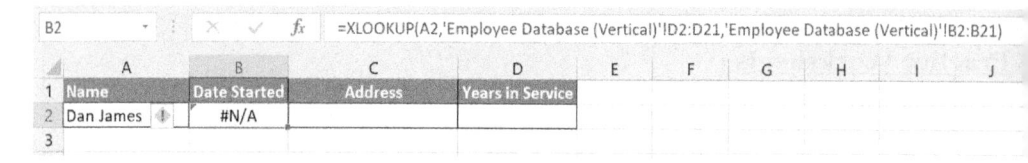

	A	B	C	D
1	Name	Date Started	Address	Years in Service
2	Dan James	#N/A		

B2 =XLOOKUP(A2,'Employee Database (Vertical)'!D2:D21,'Employee Database (Vertical)'!B2:B21)

The formula in cell B2 to enter the date started is:

=XLOOKUP(A2,'Employee Database (Vertical)'!D2:D21,'Employee Database (Vertical)'!B2:B21)

However, I get a #N/A error. This is because the name Dan James is not in the list of employee names in the **Employee Database (Vertical)** table in column D.

To overcome this, I will use the if_not_found argument. This is the fourth argument in XLOOKUP.

	A	B	C	D
1	Name	Date Started	Address	Years in Service
2	Dan James	No Data		

B2 =XLOOKUP(A2,'Employee Database (Vertical)'!D2:D21,'Employee Database (Vertical)'!B2:B21,"No Data")

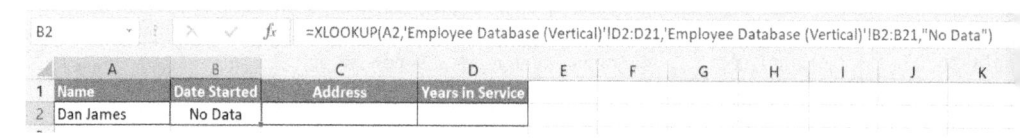

In the if_not_found argument I entered "No Data". The full formula is:

=XLOOKUP(A2,'Employee Database (Vertical)'!D2:D21,'Employee Database (Vertical)'!B2:B21,"No Data")

You can do the same in cells C2 and D2 as they will also return #N/A error if the if_not_found argument is not used.

For completeness, the formula to extract the address in cell C2 is:

=XLOOKUP(A2,'Employee Database (Vertical)'!D2:D21,'Employee Database (Vertical)'!C2:C21,"No Data")

The formula to extract the years in service in cell D2 is:

=XLOOKUP(A2,'Employee Database (Vertical)'!D2:D21,'Employee Database (Vertical)'!E2:E21,"No Data")

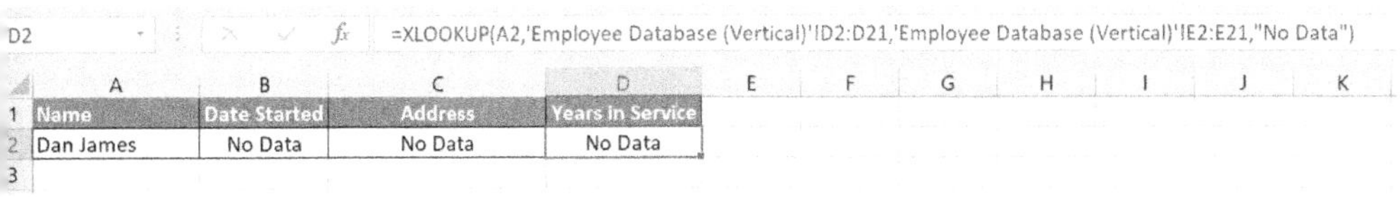

	A	B	C	D
1	Name	Date Started	Address	Years in Service
2	Dan James	No Data	No Data	No Data

This now displays "No Data" in cells B2, C2 and D2.

Additional Notes

1) Some of the more common entries for the if_not_found argument are "Not Found", "No Records", "No Match" and "No Result"

2) You must remember to enclose the text in quotation marks otherwise you will get a #NAME? error

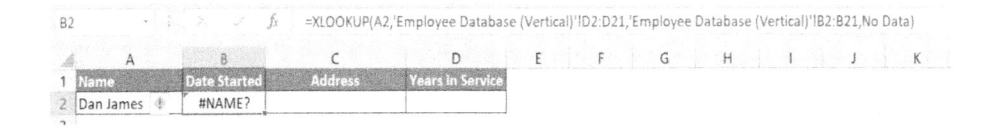

	A	B	C	D
1	Name	Date Started	Address	Years in Service
2	Dan James	#NAME?		

3) If you do not want to see any #N/A errors or text, then insert double quotation marks (" ") in the if_not_found argument. This means the cell will display nothing

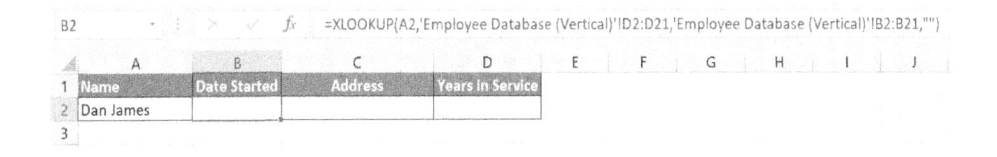

	A	B	C	D
1	Name	Date Started	Address	Years in Service
2	Dan James			

Chapter 7: How to Perform an Approximate Match with XLOOKUP

Most people will use XLOOKUP to perform an exact match but on som[e] occasions you will need to perform an approximate match. Some of th[e] most common reasons why you would use an approximate match is to giv[e] students a grade based on their test results or to calculate how much ta[x] to apply to employees based on their annual earnings. In this chapter, [I] will show you how to do an approximate match by applying a bonus t[o] each employee in the employee database based on how long they hav[e] been with the company.

Practice Worksheets

If you would like to follow along then please use the **Employee Database (Vertical)** tab and the **Chapter 7 Worksheet** tab in your practice worksheets

	A	B	C	D	E	F	G	H
1	Employee ID	Date Started	Address	Name	Years in Service		Years in Service	Loyalty Bonus
2	1011	04/09/2011	67 Tapping Close	Jim Faraday	8		2	$100
3	1015	19/02/2005	12 Brow Hill Way	Hardeep Kang	14		5	$200
4	1029	12/08/2016	19 Little Field Street	Raul Gonzalez	3		10	$400
5	1089	11/07/2014	90 Thomas Road	Liz Smith	5		15	$600
6	1105	28/04/2001	67 Pasture Street	Emma Jane	18		20	$800
7	1146	08/05/1998	145 Beacroft Avenue	Sara Kenny	21		25	$1,000
8	1178	14/04/2007	289 Price Street	Jessica Campbell	12			
9	1297	06/11/1992	128 Byron Avenue	Mick Taylor	27			
10	1356	27/12/1997	45 Wordsworth Street	Rosie Jenkins	22			
11	1398	24/01/2018	266 Long Hall Street	Michael Kane	1			
12	1404	04/10/2019	405 Milton Street	Jason Peters	0			
13	1478	14/02/2011	19 Foxes Way	Veronica Bridge	8			
14	1499	09/10/2009	99 Leyfield Cross	James Porter	10			
15	1556	18/09/2006	44 Shelley Avenue	Simon James	13			
16	1089	11/07/2014	87 Narrow Hall Way	Liz Smith	5			
17	1599	27/11/2017	72 Crossfield Street	William Gamble	2			
18	1626	21/04/2019	189 Burns Avenue	Michelle Conner	0			
19	1688	16/02/2015	52 Golds Way	Tess Kelly	4			
20	1727	09/05/2016	456 Hampton Way	Jenny Fuller	3			
21	1799	14/06/1991	288 Strand Street	Angie Greene	28			

I will use the employee database in the **Employee Database (Vertical)** tab. The table next to it in the range G1:H7 displays how much loyalty bonus to give an employee based on how long they have been with the company.

	A	B	C	D	E
1	Name	Date Started	Address	Years in Service	Loyalty Bonus
2	Angie Greene	14/06/1991	288 Strand Street	28	
3	Emma Jane	28/04/2001	67 Pasture Street	18	
4	Hardeep Kang	19/02/2005	12 Brow Hill Way	14	
5	James Porter	09/10/2009	99 Leyfield Cross	10	
6	Jason Peters	04/10/2019	405 Milton Street	0	
7	Jenny Fuller	09/05/2016	456 Hampton Way	3	
8	Jessica Campbell	14/04/2007	289 Price Street	12	
9	Jim Faraday	04/09/2011	67 Tapping Close	8	
10	Liz Smith	11/07/2014	90 Thomas Road	5	
11	Liz Smith	11/07/2014	90 Thomas Road	5	
12	Michael Kane	24/01/2018	266 Long Hall Street	1	
13	Michelle Conner	21/04/2019	189 Burns Avenue	0	
14	Mick Taylor	06/11/1992	128 Byron Avenue	27	
15	Raul Gonzalez	12/08/2016	19 Little Field Street	3	
16	Rosie Jenkins	27/12/1997	45 Wordsworth Street	22	
17	Sara Kenny	08/05/1998	145 Beacroft Avenue	21	
18	Simon James	18/09/2006	44 Shelley Avenue	13	
19	Tess Kelly	16/02/2015	52 Golds Way	4	
20	Veronica Bridge	14/02/2011	19 Foxes Way	8	
21	William Gamble	27/11/2017	72 Crossfield Street	2	

The goal is to populate column E in the **Chapter 7 Worksheet** tab using the years in service in column D as the lookup value.

E2   fx   =XLOOKUP(D2,'Employee Database (Vertical)'!$G$2:$G$7,'Employee Database (Vertical)'!$H$2:$H$7,,-1)

	A	B	C	D	E
1	Name	Date Started	Address	Years in Service	Loyalty Bonus
2	Angie Greene	14/06/1991	288 Strand Street	28	$1,000
3	Emma Jane	28/04/2001	67 Pasture Street	18	
4	Hardeep Kang	19/02/2005	12 Brow Hill Way	14	
5	James Porter	09/10/2009	99 Leyfield Cross	10	
6	Jason Peters	04/10/2019	405 Milton Street	0	
7	Jenny Fuller	09/05/2016	456 Hampton Way	3	
8	Jessica Campbell	14/04/2007	289 Price Street	12	
9	Jim Faraday	04/09/2011	67 Tapping Close	8	
10	Liz Smith	11/07/2014	90 Thomas Road	5	
11	Liz Smith	11/07/2014	90 Thomas Road	5	
12	Michael Kane	24/01/2018	266 Long Hall Street	1	
13	Michelle Conner	21/04/2019	189 Burns Avenue	0	
14	Mick Taylor	06/11/1992	128 Byron Avenue	27	
15	Raul Gonzalez	12/08/2016	19 Little Field Street	3	
16	Rosie Jenkins	27/12/1997	45 Wordsworth Street	22	
17	Sara Kenny	08/05/1998	145 Beacroft Avenue	21	
18	Simon James	18/09/2006	44 Shelley Avenue	13	
19	Tess Kelly	16/02/2015	52 Golds Way	4	
20	Veronica Bridge	14/02/2011	19 Foxes Way	8	
21	William Gamble	27/11/2017	72 Crossfield Street	2	

The formula in cell E2 is:

=XLOOKUP(D2,'Employee Database (Vertical)'!$G$2:$G$7,'Employee Database (Vertical)'!$H$2:$H$7,,-1)

I will break this formula down by its arguments to explain how this works:

lookup_value – The lookup value is the years in service, so it is cell D2 in the **Chapter 7 Worksheet** tab

lookup_array – The lookup array is the years in service column in the **Employee Database (Vertical)** tab in the range G2:G7

return_array – The return array is how much loyalty bonus to give each employee which is in the range H2:H7 in the **Employee Database (Vertical)** tab

if_not_found – I have skipped this argument by entering a comma (,)

match_mode – In this argument you can select one of four choices. These are:

1) 0 - Exact match
2) -1 - Exact match or next smaller item
3) 1 - Exact match or next larger item
4) 2 - Wildcard character match

Years in Service	Loyalty Bonus
2	$100
5	$200
10	$400
15	$600
20	$800
25	$1,000

I want to extract the value which is the next smaller item, so I choose **-1 - Exact match or next smaller item**. This means that if a value falls between two milestones, it would select the smaller of the two. For example, if an employee has been at the company for 3 years, then they will get a bonus of $100 because this falls between 2 and 5 years and the smaller of the two milestones is 2 years so it selects $100. If an employee has worked for 22 years at the company then they will get a bonus of $800 because this sits between 20 and 25 years and the smaller of the two is 20 years so it selects $800.

E2: `=XLOOKUP(D2,'Employee Database (Vertical)'!$G$2:$G$7,'Employee Database (Vertical)'!$H$2:$H$7,,1)`

	Name	Date Started	Address	Years in Service	Loyalty Bonus
2	Angie Greene	14/06/1991	288 Strand Street	28	#N/A
3	Emma Jane	28/04/2001	67 Pasture Street	18	$800
4	Hardeep Kang	19/02/2005	12 Brow Hill Way	14	$600
5	James Porter	09/10/2009	99 Leyfield Cross	10	$400
6	Jason Peters	04/10/2019	405 Milton Street	0	$100
7	Jenny Fuller	09/05/2016	456 Hampton Way	3	$200
8	Jessica Campbell	14/04/2007	289 Price Street	12	$600
9	Jim Faraday	04/09/2011	67 Tapping Close	8	$400
10	Liz Smith	11/07/2014	90 Thomas Road	5	$200
11	Liz Smith	11/07/2014	90 Thomas Road	5	$200
12	Michael Kane	24/01/2018	266 Long Hall Street	1	$100
13	Michelle Conner	21/04/2019	189 Burns Avenue	0	$100
14	Mick Taylor	06/11/1992	128 Byron Avenue	27	#N/A
15	Raul Gonzalez	12/08/2016	19 Little Field Street	3	$200
16	Rosie Jenkins	27/12/1997	45 Wordsworth Street	22	$1,000
17	Sara Kenny	08/05/1998	145 Beacroft Avenue	21	$1,000
18	Simon James	18/09/2006	44 Shelley Avenue	13	$600
19	Tess Kelly	16/02/2015	52 Golds Way	4	$200
20	Veronica Bridge	14/02/2011	19 Foxes Way	8	$400
21	William Gamble	27/11/2017	72 Crossfield Street	2	$100

If I chose **1 - Exact match or next larger item** and copied the formula down, then I would get the above results in column E. This means if the lookup value falls between two milestones it would choose the higher of the two. For example, if the employee has worked for 3 years at the company then it would select $200 because this falls between 2 and 5 years and the larger of the two milestones is 5 years so it selects $200.

E2 =XLOOKUP(D2,'Employee Database (Vertical)'!$G$2:$G$7,'Employee Database (Vertical)'!$H$2:$H$7,,-1)

	A	B	C	D	E
1	Name	Date Started	Address	Years in Service	Loyalty Bonus
2	Angie Greene	14/06/1991	288 Strand Street	28	$1,000
3	Emma Jane	28/04/2001	67 Pasture Street	18	$600
4	Hardeep Kang	19/02/2005	12 Brow Hill Way	14	$400
5	James Porter	09/10/2009	99 Leyfield Cross	10	$400
6	Jason Peters	04/10/2019	405 Milton Street	0	#N/A
7	Jenny Fuller	09/05/2016	456 Hampton Way	3	$100
8	Jessica Campbell	14/04/2007	289 Price Street	12	$400
9	Jim Faraday	04/09/2011	67 Tapping Close	8	$200
10	Liz Smith	11/07/2014	90 Thomas Road	5	$200
11	Liz Smith	11/07/2014	90 Thomas Road	5	$200
12	Michael Kane	24/01/2018	266 Long Hall Street	1	#N/A
13	Michelle Conner	21/04/2019	189 Burns Avenue	0	#N/A
14	Mick Taylor	06/11/1992	128 Byron Avenue	27	$1,000
15	Raul Gonzalez	12/08/2016	19 Little Field Street	3	$100
16	Rosie Jenkins	27/12/1997	45 Wordsworth Street	22	$800
17	Sara Kenny	08/05/1998	145 Beacroft Avenue	21	$800
18	Simon James	18/09/2006	44 Shelley Avenue	13	$400
19	Tess Kelly	16/02/2015	52 Golds Way	4	$100
20	Veronica Bridge	14/02/2011	19 Foxes Way	8	$200
21	William Gamble	27/11/2017	72 Crossfield Street	2	$100

The correct way to do this is by selecting **-1 - Exact match or next smaller item**. I do not need to enter anything in the search_mode argument so I close the bracket. I then copied the formula down to cell E21 to get the above results in column E.

Sorting the Data Table

An important point to make is that you do not need to sort the data table in ascending or descending order before you do an approximate match. It will still give you the correct results.

Years in Service	Loyalty Bonus
5	$200
20	$800
2	$100
15	$600
25	$1,000
10	$400

For example, I have sorted the above table in a random order.

	A	B	C	D	E
1	Name	Date Started	Address	Years in Service	Loyalty Bonus
2	Angie Greene	14/06/1991	288 Strand Street	28	$1,000
3	Emma Jane	28/04/2001	67 Pasture Street	18	$600
4	Hardeep Kang	19/02/2005	12 Brow Hill Way	14	$400
5	James Porter	09/10/2009	99 Leyfield Cross	10	$400
6	Jason Peters	04/10/2019	405 Milton Street	0	#N/A
7	Jenny Fuller	09/05/2016	456 Hampton Way	3	$100
8	Jessica Campbell	14/04/2007	289 Price Street	12	$400
9	Jim Faraday	04/09/2011	67 Tapping Close	8	$200
10	Liz Smith	11/07/2014	90 Thomas Road	5	$200
11	Liz Smith	11/07/2014	90 Thomas Road	5	$200
12	Michael Kane	24/01/2018	266 Long Hall Street	1	#N/A
13	Michelle Conner	21/04/2019	189 Burns Avenue	0	#N/A
14	Mick Taylor	06/11/1992	128 Byron Avenue	27	$1,000
15	Raul Gonzalez	12/08/2016	19 Little Field Street	3	$100
16	Rosie Jenkins	27/12/1997	45 Wordsworth Street	22	$800
17	Sara Kenny	08/05/1998	145 Beacroft Avenue	21	$800
18	Simon James	18/09/2006	44 Shelley Avenue	13	$400
19	Tess Kelly	16/02/2015	52 Golds Way	4	$100
20	Veronica Bridge	14/02/2011	19 Foxes Way	8	$200
21	William Gamble	27/11/2017	72 Crossfield Street	2	$100

As you can see above, it still gives the correct results in column E.

Handling Errors in an Approximate Match

Notice there are some #N/A errors for the employees who have been at the company under 2 years. This is because the loyalty bonus starts when an employee has worked for a minimum of 2 years in the range G2:G7 in the **Employee Database (Vertical)** tab.

	A	B	C	D	E
1	Name	Date Started	Address	Years in Service	Loyalty Bonus
2	Angie Greene	14/06/1991	288 Strand Street	28	$1,000
3	Emma Jane	28/04/2001	67 Pasture Street	18	$600
4	Hardeep Kang	19/02/2005	12 Brow Hill Way	14	$400
5	James Porter	09/10/2009	99 Leyfield Cross	10	$400
6	Jason Peters	04/10/2019	405 Milton Street	0	No Bonus
7	Jenny Fuller	09/05/2016	456 Hampton Way	3	$100
8	Jessica Campbell	14/04/2007	289 Price Street	12	$400
9	Jim Faraday	04/09/2011	67 Tapping Close	8	$200
10	Liz Smith	11/07/2014	90 Thomas Road	5	$200
11	Liz Smith	11/07/2014	90 Thomas Road	5	$200
12	Michael Kane	24/01/2018	266 Long Hall Street	1	No Bonus
13	Michelle Conner	21/04/2019	189 Burns Avenue	0	No Bonus
14	Mick Taylor	06/11/1992	128 Byron Avenue	27	$1,000
15	Raul Gonzalez	12/08/2016	19 Little Field Street	3	$100
16	Rosie Jenkins	27/12/1997	45 Wordsworth Street	22	$800
17	Sara Kenny	08/05/1998	145 Beacroft Avenue	21	$800
18	Simon James	18/09/2006	44 Shelley Avenue	13	$400
19	Tess Kelly	16/02/2015	52 Golds Way	4	$100
20	Veronica Bridge	14/02/2011	19 Foxes Way	8	$200
21	William Gamble	27/11/2017	72 Crossfield Street	2	$100

To overcome this, you can insert some text in the if_not_found argument to make the table look cleaner as explained in chapter 6. In this example I entered "No Bonus" in the if_not_found argument.

The complete formula in cell E2 is:

=XLOOKUP(D2,'Employee Database (Vertical)'!$G$2:$G$7,'Employee Database (Vertical)'!$H$2:$H$7,"No Bonus",-1)

Chapter 8: Perform Partial Matches with XLOOKUP

As with VLOOKUP and HLOOKUP you can use wildcards to perform "fuzzy" matches on text. A wildcard is a special character that lets you do partial matches. There are three wildcards in total.

Excel Wildcard Characters

The three wildcard characters are:

1) **Asterisk (*)** – This represents any number of characters before or after a text. For example, Emp* can return Employee, Employment, Employed, Empathy. An asterisk can be placed at the beginning of a text such as *ing. This would return any number of characters before ing such as playing, doing, counting and so on

2) **Question mark (?)** – This represents just a single character. For example, C?t can return Cat, Cot, Cut. A question mark (?) is used to be more specific while still not being exact

3) **Tilde (~)** – This is used to identify a wildcard character (*,?,~) in a text. For example, if a text string contains a question mark (?) as part of the text string, then by adding a tilde (~), Excel will ignore the question mark as a wildcard

How to do a Partial Match with XLOOKUP

The key to performing a partial match in XLOOKUP is to select the number 2 in the match_mode argument.

Practice Worksheets

If you would like to follow along then please use the **Employee Database (Vertical)** tab and the **Chapter 8 Worksheet** tab in your practice worksheets

	A	B	C	D	E
1	Employee ID	Date Started	Address	Name	Years in Service
2	1011	04/09/2011	67 Tapping Close	Jim Faraday	8
3	1015	19/02/2005	12 Brow Hill Way	Hardeep Kang	14
4	1029	12/08/2016	19 Little Field Street	Raul Gonzalez	3
5	1089	11/07/2014	90 Thomas Road	Liz Smith	5
6	1105	28/04/2001	67 Pasture Street	Emma Jane	18
7	1146	08/05/1998	145 Beacroft Avenue	Sara Kenny	21
8	1178	14/04/2007	289 Price Street	Jessica Campbell	12
9	1297	06/11/1992	128 Byron Avenue	Mick Taylor	27
10	1356	27/12/1997	45 Wordsworth Street	Rosie Jenkins	22
11	1398	24/01/2018	266 Long Hall Street	Michael Kane	1
12	1404	04/10/2019	405 Milton Street	Jason Peters	0
13	1478	14/02/2011	19 Foxes Way	Veronica Bridge	8
14	1499	09/10/2009	99 Leyfield Cross	James Porter	10
15	1556	18/09/2006	44 Shelley Avenue	Simon James	13
16	1089	11/07/2014	87 Narrow Hall Way	Liz Smith	5
17	1599	27/11/2017	72 Crossfield Street	William Gamble	2
18	1626	21/04/2019	189 Burns Avenue	Michelle Conner	0
19	1688	16/02/2015	52 Golds Way	Tess Kelly	4
20	1727	09/05/2016	456 Hampton Way	Jenny Fuller	3
21	1799	14/06/1991	288 Strand Street	Angie Greene	28

Let us have a look at an example of how to perform a partial match using the employee database in the **Employee Database (Vertical)** tab.

	A	B	C	D
1	Name		Search	
2			Ver*	
3				

I want to extract the name of the person that starts with "Ver" and enter this in cell A2 in the **Chapter 8 Worksheet** tab. The lookup value is in cell C2. Notice the asterisk (*) after "Ver". Remember, this means extracting any number of characters before or after a text. In this case, it is any number of characters after "Ver".

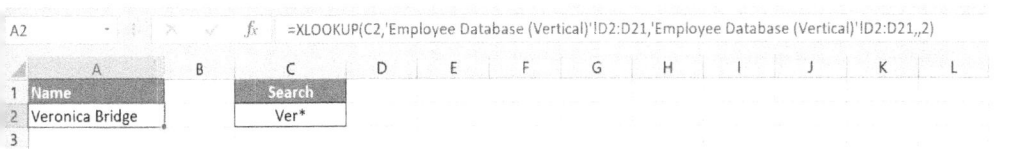

	A	B	C	D	E	F	G	H	I	J	K	L
			fx	=XLOOKUP(C2,'Employee Database (Vertical)'!D2:D21,'Employee Database (Vertical)'!D2:D21,,2)								
1	Name		Search									
2	Veronica Bridge		Ver*									
3												

The XLOOKUP formula in cell A2 in the **Chapter 8 Worksheet** tab is:

=XLOOKUP(C2,'Employee Database (Vertical)'!D2:D21,'Employee Database (Vertical)'!D2:D21,,2)

To explain how this formula works I will break it down by its arguments:

lookup_value – The lookup value is the partial name in cell C2 in the **Chapter 8 Worksheet** tab

lookup_array – The lookup array are the names in the **Employee Database (Vertical)** tab in the range D2:D21

return_array – The return array are also the names in the **Employee Database (Vertical)** tab in the range D2:D21 because I want to return the employee name

if_not_found – I have skipped this argument by entering a comma (,)

match_mode – As mentioned in the previous chapter, there are 4 options to choose from. You need to select **2 - Wildcard character match**

Let's have a look at another example of performing a partial match with wildcard character.

	A	B	C	D
1	Name		Search	
2	Veronica Bridge		Ver*	
3				
4				
5	Name		Search	
6			*Kelly	
7				

In this example, I want to extract the name of the person whose last name is "Kelly" and enter it in cell A6 in the **Chapter 8 Worksheet** tab. Notice the asterisk (*) is before the last name this time.

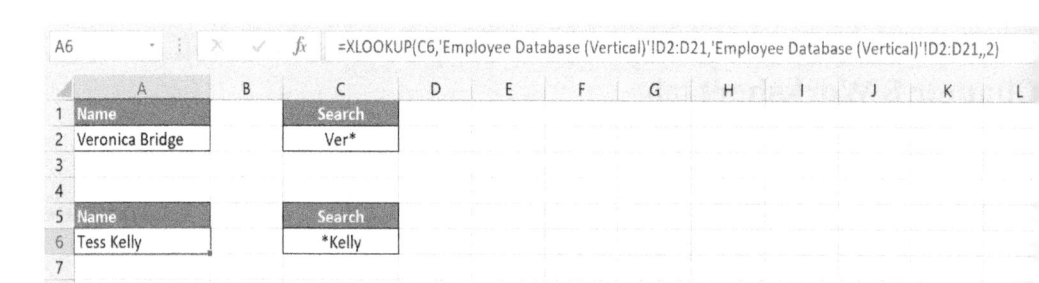

	A	B	C	D	E	F	G	H	I	J	K	L
1	Name		Search									
2	Veronica Bridge		Ver*									
3												
4												
5	Name		Search									
6	Tess Kelly		*Kelly									
7												

The formula in cell A6 is:

=XLOOKUP(C6,'Employee Database (Vertical)'!D2:D21,'Employee Database (Vertical)'!D2:D21,,2)

This formula works in the same way as the previous one. The only difference is where the position of the asterisk (*) was located.

Chapter 9: How to Extract the Last Value with XLOOKUP

One of the great features of XLOOKUP is the ability in how it searches. As well as searching from the top to the bottom of a column, XLOOKUP can also search from the bottom to the top of a column and extract the last value. With VLOOKUP, it only looks from the top to the bottom and extract the first value. To change how XLOOKUP performs its search you enter a value in the search_mode argument.

The Search_Mode Argument

The search_mode argument has four options to choose from which I have explained in chapter 1 but to recap:

1) **1 - Search first-to-last** – This is the default and XLOOKUP starts searching from the top row and works its way down to find the first match

2) **-1 - Search last-to-first** – XLOOKUP starts searching from the bottom row and works its way up to find the first match. This is useful if you want to extract the last value

3) **2 - Binary search (sorted ascending order)** – This performs a binary search. The data needs to be sorted in ascending order first otherwise XLOOKUP can return an error or a wrong result. The system compares each cell to the middle value in the column and if it doesn't match then it searches further

4) **-2 - Binary search (sorted descending order)** – This performs a binary search. The data needs to be sorted in descending order first otherwise XLOOKUP can return an error or a wrong result. The system compares each cell to the middle value in the column and if it does not match then it searches further

Extracting the Last Value

The most common reason why you would use the search_mode argument other than extracting the first value is it to extract the last value. I will give you an example of how to do this using the employee database in the **Employee Database (Vertical)** tab.

> **Practice Worksheets**
>
> If you would like to follow along then please use the **Employee Database (Vertical)** tab and the **Chapter 9 Worksheet** tab in your practice worksheets

	A	B	C	D	E
1	Employee ID	Date Started	Address	Name	Years in Service
2	1011	04/09/2011	67 Tapping Close	Jim Faraday	8
3	1015	19/02/2005	12 Brow Hill Way	Hardeep Kang	14
4	1029	12/08/2016	19 Little Field Street	Raul Gonzalez	3
5	1089	11/07/2014	90 Thomas Road	Liz Smith	5
6	1105	28/04/2001	67 Pasture Street	Emma Jane	18
7	1146	08/05/1998	145 Beacroft Avenue	Sara Kenny	21
8	1178	14/04/2007	289 Price Street	Jessica Campbell	12
9	1297	06/11/1992	128 Byron Avenue	Mick Taylor	27
10	1356	27/12/1997	45 Wordsworth Street	Rosie Jenkins	22
11	1398	24/01/2018	266 Long Hall Street	Michael Kane	1
12	1404	04/10/2019	405 Milton Street	Jason Peters	0
13	1478	14/02/2011	19 Foxes Way	Veronica Bridge	8
14	1499	09/10/2009	99 Leyfield Cross	James Porter	10
15	1556	18/09/2006	44 Shelley Avenue	Simon James	13
16	1089	11/07/2014	87 Narrow Hall Way	Liz Smith	5
17	1599	27/11/2017	72 Crossfield Street	William Gamble	2
18	1626	21/04/2019	189 Burns Avenue	Michelle Conner	0
19	1688	16/02/2015	52 Golds Way	Tess Kelly	4
20	1727	09/05/2016	456 Hampton Way	Jenny Fuller	3
21	1799	14/06/1991	288 Strand Street	Angie Greene	28

In the employee database in the **Employee Database (Vertical)** tab there are two entries for Liz Smith. This is because she has moved address since she first started working for the company.

	A	B	C	D	E	F
1	Name	Date Started	Address	Years in Service	Loyalty Bonus	
2	Liz Smith	11/07/2014		5	$200	
3						

In the **Chapter 9 Worksheet** tab in cell C2 I want to extract her current address "87 Narrow Hall Way" and not "90 Thomas Road" which is her old address. To do this, I need to change how XLOOKUP performs its search using the search_mode argument.

C2 fx =XLOOKUP(A2,'Employee Database (Vertical)'!D2:D21,'Employee Database (Vertical)'!C2:C21,,,-1)

	A	B	C	D	E	F	G	H	I	J	K
1	Name	Date Started	Address	Years in Service	Loyalty Bonus						
2	Liz Smith	11/07/2014	87 Narrow Hall Way	5	$200						
3											

The formula in cell C2 is:

=XLOOKUP(A2,'Employee Database (Vertical)'!D2:D21,'Employee Database (Vertical)'!C2:C21,,,-1)

I will explain how the formula works below:

lookup_value – The lookup value is the employee name "Liz Smith" in cell A2 in the **Chapter 9 Worksheet** tab

lookup_array – The lookup array are the names in the **Employee Database (Vertical)** tab in the range D2:D21

return_array – The return array is the address in the **Employee Database (Vertical)** tab in the range C2:C21 because I want to return the address

if_not_found – I have skipped this argument by entering a comma (,)

match_mode – I have skipped this argument by entering a comma (,)

search_mode – I want XLOOKUP to search from bottom to the top, so I select **-1 - Search last-to-first**

As you can see, the search_mode argument can be very useful when you want to extract the most up to date information.

Chapter 10: Extracting Multiple Values with XLOOKUP

Another great feature of XLOOKUP is the ability to extract multiple values with the same formula. This can make you more efficient and save you time as you do not have to create multiple formulas in different cells.

Now let's look at an example of how to do this.

Practice Worksheets

If you would like to follow along then please use the **Employee Database (Vertical)** tab and the **Chapter 10 Worksheet** tab in your practice worksheets

	A	B	C	D	E
1	Employee ID	Date Started	Address	Name	Years in Service
2	1011	04/09/2011	67 Tapping Close	Jim Faraday	8
3	1015	19/02/2005	12 Brow Hill Way	Hardeep Kang	14
4	1029	12/08/2016	19 Little Field Street	Raul Gonzalez	3
5	1089	11/07/2014	90 Thomas Road	Liz Smith	5
6	1105	28/04/2001	67 Pasture Street	Emma Jane	18
7	1146	08/05/1998	145 Beacroft Avenue	Sara Kenny	21
8	1178	14/04/2007	289 Price Street	Jessica Campbell	12
9	1297	06/11/1992	128 Byron Avenue	Mick Taylor	27
10	1356	27/12/1997	45 Wordsworth Street	Rosie Jenkins	22
11	1398	24/01/2018	266 Long Hall Street	Michael Kane	1
12	1404	04/10/2019	405 Milton Street	Jason Peters	0
13	1478	14/02/2011	19 Foxes Way	Veronica Bridge	8
14	1499	09/10/2009	99 Leyfield Cross	James Porter	10
15	1556	18/09/2006	44 Shelley Avenue	Simon James	13
16	1089	11/07/2014	87 Narrow Hall Way	Liz Smith	5
17	1599	27/11/2017	72 Crossfield Street	William Gamble	2
18	1626	21/04/2019	189 Burns Avenue	Michelle Conner	0
19	1688	16/02/2015	52 Golds Way	Tess Kelly	4
20	1727	09/05/2016	456 Hampton Way	Jenny Fuller	3
21	1799	14/06/1991	288 Strand Street	Angie Greene	28

As with the previous chapters, I will use the employee database in the **Employee Database (Vertical)** tab.

	A	B	C	D	E	F
1	Employee ID	Date Started	Address	Name	Years in Service	
2	1356					
3						

In the **Chapter 11 Worksheet** tab, I want to enter the date started, address, name of the employee and the number of years' service for employee ID 1356 in the range B2:E2 with just a single formula.

Here are the steps on how to do this:

1) Select the range where you want the values to be in. In this example the values will be in the range B2:E2 so I select this range

	A	B	C	D	E	F
1	Employee ID	Date Started	Address	Name	Years in Service	
2	1356					
3						

2) You now need to enter the formula. The formula to enter is:

=XLOOKUP(A2,'Employee Database (Vertical)'!A2:A21,'Employee Database (Vertical)'!B2:E21)

Here is a breakdown of this formula by its arguments:

lookup_value – This is the employee ID number in cell A2 in the **Chapter 10 Worksheet** tab

lookup_array – This is the employee ID column in the **Employee Database (Vertical)** tab which is the range A2:A21

return_array – These are the values from the columns I want to return. I want to extract the values in the date started, address name, and years in service columns so I select the range B2:E21 in the **Employee Database (Vertical)** tab

3) Once you press Enter on your keyboard the four values are returned and spilled into the range B2:E2

	A	B	C	D	E
1	Employee ID	Date Started	Address	Name	Years in Service
2	1356	27/12/1997	45 Wordsworth Street	Rosie Jenkins	22
3					

B2# formula: =XLOOKUP(A2,'Employee Database (Vertical)'!A2:A21,'Employee Database (Vertical)'!B2:E21)

What is Spilled?

You will also get the following message saying the formula has been spilled, but what does the term "spilled" mean?

Formula spilled
Your formula returned multiple values, so we spilled them into the neighboring blank cells.

Spill occurs whenever you create a formula that return multiple results. Excel "spills" these results into multiple cells automatically. In the above example, even though the formula was created just once, the four values were spilled into cells B2, C2, D2 and E2.

If something on the worksheet blocks a spilled array formula, Excel will return a #SPILL! error.

Note:

Spilling is only available in Office 365

Chapter 11: How to Perform Two-Way Lookups

XLOOKUP can be nested inside another XLOOKUP to perform two-way lookups. Two-way lookups are very powerful, and it searches values in a row and column to return a value from an array. Normally, you would use the INDEX+MATCH functions to perform this feat but you can easily perform this with XLOOKUP as well.

Practice Worksheets

If you would like to follow along then please use the **Chapter 11 Worksheet** tab in your practice worksheets

Let us now look at an example of how to perform a two-way lookup with XLOOKUP.

	A	B	C	D	E	F	G	H	I	J	K	L	M
1		Jan	Feb	Mar	Apr	May	Jun	Jul	Aug	Sep	Oct	Nov	Dec
2	Jim Faraday	$991	$520	$815	$189	$512	$880	$603	$986	$720	$331	$255	$334
3	Hardeep Kang	$917	$499	$235	$522	$670	$584	$58	$56	$812	$752	$473	$824
4	Raul Gonzalez	$316	$793	$955	$312	$222	$647	$973	$724	$963	$856	$432	$723
5	Liz Smith	$614	$841	$694	$702	$276	$150	$859	$330	$203	$863	$193	$798
6	Emma Jane	$707	$560	$782	$868	$301	$934	$275	$514	$617	$282	$212	$869
7	Sara Kenny	$289	$677	$457	$999	$275	$772	$825	$741	$800	$810	$790	$286
8	Jessica Campbell	$2	$341	$379	$44	$619	$753	$299	$858	$41	$608	$610	$231
9	Mick Taylor	$646	$283	$398	$634	$710	$667	$508	$869	$628	$483	$565	$147
10	Rosie Jenkins	$732	$472	$405	$438	$970	$263	$457	$452	$220	$940	$911	$730
11	Michael Kane	$969	$294	$63	$109	$606	$112	$496	$38	$359	$586	$311	$889
12	Jason Peters	$915	$117	$106	$928	$602	$632	$504	$453	$504	$701	$233	$278
13	Veronica Bridge	$258	$27	$438	$847	$935	$65	$882	$741	$926	$395	$467	$967
14	James Porter	$643	$501	$256	$544	$50	$476	$186	$919	$423	$529	$888	$947
15													
16	Name	Mick Taylor											
17	Month	Jul											
18	Sales												

In the above example, there is a list of sales people along with their sales in each month in the range A1:M14 in the **Chapter 11 Worksheet** tab. In cell B18, I want to extract the sales for Mick Taylor in the month of July.

	A	B	C	D	E	F	G	H	I	J	K	L	M
1		Jan	Feb	Mar	Apr	May	Jun	Jul	Aug	Sep	Oct	Nov	Dec
2	Jim Faraday	$991	$520	$815	$189	$512	$880	$603	$986	$720	$331	$255	$334
3	Hardeep Kang	$917	$499	$235	$522	$670	$584	$58	$56	$812	$752	$473	$824
4	Raul Gonzalez	$316	$793	$955	$312	$222	$647	$973	$724	$963	$856	$432	$723
5	Liz Smith	$614	$841	$694	$702	$276	$150	$859	$330	$203	$863	$193	$798
6	Emma Jane	$707	$560	$782	$868	$301	$934	$275	$514	$617	$282	$212	$869
7	Sara Kenny	$289	$677	$457	$999	$275	$772	$825	$741	$800	$810	$790	$286
8	Jessica Campbell	$2	$341	$379	$44	$619	$753	$299	$858	$41	$608	$610	$231
9	Mick Taylor	$646	$283	$398	$634	$710	$667	$508	$869	$628	$483	$565	$147
10	Rosie Jenkins	$732	$472	$405	$438	$970	$263	$457	$452	$220	$940	$911	$730
11	Michael Kane	$969	$294	$63	$109	$606	$112	$496	$38	$359	$586	$311	$889
12	Jason Peters	$915	$117	$106	$928	$602	$632	$504	$453	$504	$701	$233	$278
13	Veronica Bridge	$258	$27	$438	$847	$935	$65	$882	$741	$926	$395	$467	$967
14	James Porter	$643	$501	$256	$544	$50	$476	$186	$919	$423	$529	$888	$947
15													
16	Name	Mick Taylor											
17	Month	Jul											
18	Sales	$508											

The formula in cell B18 is:

=XLOOKUP(B16,A2:A14,XLOOKUP(B17,B1:M1,B2:M14))

I will break this formula down by its arguments to explain how this two-way lookup formula works:

1st XLOOKUP

lookup_value – In the first XLOOKUP, I want to search for the name "Mick Taylor", so the lookup value is cell B16

lookup_array – I want to search the name "Mick Taylor" in the range A2:A14 as this is where the list of sales people are

return_array – In this argument I insert another XLOOKUP function so I can do a column search

2nd XLOOKUP

lookup_value – In the second XLOOKUP, I want to search for the month "Jul", so the lookup value is cell B17

lookup_array – I want to look up the month "Jul" in the range B1:M1 as this is where the list of months is

return_array – The return array is the array of sales in the range B2:M14

I do not need the optional arguments, if_not_found, match_mode and search_mode so I close the brackets after the return_array argument.

So how does this formula work? This formula first searches the name of the salesperson in the range A2:A14 and locates the row index number for Mick Taylor. This is in row 8 of the range A2:A14. It then does a search of the month and locates the column index number for Jul in the range B1:M1. Jul is in column 7 of the range B1:M1. It then does a cross section between row 8 and column 7 and returns $508.

About the Author

I'm Harjit Suman and I love all things Excel. I wrote this book as I want to teach you all about Excel and its vast arrange of tools and features to enable you to become as efficient as possible with your spreadsheets. really enjoyed learning Excel over the years and picked up vast amount of knowledge in this awesome spreadsheet program. I now want to pas on my knowledge to you and my goal is to make this an enjoyable learning experience for you too.

My Background

The first time I used Excel was in my first analytical role as a Business Analyst back in 2008. The problem was, I had no great experience in Excel other than simple data entry. Some of my first projects in data analysis took so long to do. In fact, most of it was manually done as I knew of no other way.

I knew this couldn't continue so I invested in a beginners Excel book to expand my knowledge. I wanted to automate my spreadsheets as much a I could to save me time. After reading my first book I started to understand the power of Excel. I bought more and more Excel books and practiced what I read in the evenings and weekends, well, whenever I had free time I then applied what I learnt in my full-time work as a Business Analyst

Soon, over time I went from an Excel beginner to an advanced user and I managed to automate my spreadsheets as much as I could.

However, I wanted to take my Excel skills to another level so I learnt Visual Basic for Applications (VBA) where I could write my own macros. I bought VBA books and practiced what I learnt in my spare time. Now I am able to write my own macros to build tools and applications not just for myself but for other businesses too.

Now it's your Turn

Over the years I have learnt a lot about Excel and I now want to pass on my knowledge to you through this book. I have also created a website, www.excelmasterconsultant.com. In here you can find reviews of the many Excel books I have read which have taken my Excel skills to the next level, and they will for you too. You will also find great tutorials and blogs I have written as well as Excel courses and add-ins you can buy. I also run an Excel consultancy service if you need any help with your spreadsheets.

I hope you enjoy this book. I would love to hear from you with anything Excel related so please get in touch by contacting me through my website.

In the meantime, happy Excel learning.

Harjit Suman

Excel Master Consultant

Additional Resources

For more information about Excel you can visit my website www.excelmasterconsultant.com.

In my website you will find:

- Excel tutorials and blogs to expand your Excel knowledge

- Books you can buy that I read while I was learning Excel which have helped me to advance my Excel skills and which I recommend to you

- Excel applications you can buy which will make you more efficient and save you time

- Online Excel and VBA courses you can buy

- More information about my Excel consultancy services that I offer

- An online shop where you can buy books, applications and courses

Please take a visit and drop me a message. I would love to hear from you.

More Books by Excel Master Consultant

If you enjoyed reading this book then please look out for more Excel books written by me. I have written Excel books in two series which are **Excel Bible for Beginners** and **Excel Formulas and Functions**.

Excel Formulas and Functions Series

Below are more books in the Excel Formulas and Functions series.

Excel Formulas and Functions: The Complete Excel Guide for Beginners

If you want to learn about the best and most commonly used Excel formulas and functions to use for your worksheets then you need to buy

Excel Formulas and Functions: The Complete Excel Guide for Beginners

This book includes:

- Tips on how to create more efficient formulas
- How the order of operator precedence in Excel formulas work
- How to check formulas in your worksheets
- How to use the Excel Insert Function Formula Builder to make formulas easier to write
- How relative, absolute and mixed cell references are used to construct formulas
- How to create sum and counting formulas using Excel functions such as SUMIF, SUMIFS, COUNTIF, COUNTIFS, COUNTBLANK
- How to create logical formulas using the IF, OR, AND functions
- How to create lookup formulas using Excel functions such as VLOOKUP, HLOOKUP and combining the INDEX and MATCH functions together to create powerful one way and two-way lookups
- How to create text formulas by using Excel functions such as LEFT, RIGHT, MID, and CONCATENATE to manipulate text in your worksheets
- Great Excel hints and tips to help you become more efficient and save time
- And much more!

You can buy the book from Amazon by entering either of the links below to your web browser:

Amazon US:

www.amazon.com/Excel-Formulas-Functions-Complete-Beginners/dp/1699170932

Amazon UK:

www.amazon.co.uk/Excel-Formulas-Functions-Complete-Beginners/dp/1699170932

Excel Formulas and Functions: The Step by Step Excel Guide on how to Create Powerful Formulas

If you want to learn how to create powerful formulas such as array formulas that perform the impossible then you can buy *Excel Formulas and Functions: The Step by Step Excel Guide on how to Create Powerful Formulas*

In this book you will learn:

- How to create more advanced Excel formulas using powerful Excel functions such as SUMPRODUCT
- How to create array formulas

- The advantages and disadvantages of array formulas
- What arrays and array constants are
- What the order of operator precedence is and how Excel orders the calculation in formulas
- How to create formulas that do the impossible!
- And much more!

Each example of how to create a formula starts off with a real-life business case scenario and will explain what Excel functions will be used in the formula to solve the business case scenario problem. It will also give you step by step instructions of how the formulas work by breaking each section of the formula down in simple easy to follow steps.

You can buy the book from Amazon by entering either of the links below to your web browser:

Amazon US:

www.amazon.com/Excel-Formulas-Functions-Create-Powerful/dp/B0863S1948

Amazon UK:

www.amazon.co.uk/Excel-Formulas-Functions-Create-Powerful/dp/B0863S1948

Excel Bible for Beginners Series

Below are books in the Excel Bible for Beginners series.

Excel Bible for Beginners: The Essential Step by Step Guide to Learn Excel for Beginners

If you are an Excel novice and would like to know all the great tools and features Excel has to offer then *Excel Bible for Beginners: The Essential Step by Step Guide to Learn Excel for Beginners* will show you.

What you will learn in this book:

- What is Excel?
- What is Excel used for?
- How to open and save workbooks
- How to use the Quick Access Toolbar
- How to change font styles

- How to wrap and merge text
- How to format numbers
- How to apply borders
- How to apply cell styles
- How to use the Format Painter tool
- How to insert and delete worksheets tabs
- How to insert and delete columns and rows
- How to freeze rows and columns
- How to hide/unhide columns and rows
- How to copy, paste and cut
- How to use the Excel Find and Replace tool
- How to use the Excel Text to Speech function
- How to create charts and format them
- How to create formulas
- How to print
- And much more!

You can buy the book from Amazon by entering either of the links below to your web browser:

Amazon US:

www.amazon.com/Excel-Bible-Beginners-Essential-Guide/dp/B088JS6YVS

Amazon UK:

www.amazon.co.uk/Excel-Bible-Beginners-Essential-Guide/dp/B088JS6YVS

Excel Bible for Beginners: The Step by Step Guide to Create Pivot Tables to Perform Excel Data Analysis and Data Crunching

If you are want to learn how to create pivot tables to easily analyse large data sets then *Excel Bible for Beginners: The Step by Step Guide to Create Pivot Tables to Perform Excel Data Analysis and Data Crunching* will teach you how.

Here are some of the topics you will learn from this Excel book:

- What is a pivot table?
- Why you should use pivot tables?
- How you should structure your data source before you create a pivot table?
- How to create a basic pivot table?
- How to format and customise a pivot table?
- How to apply number formatting to a pivot table?
- How to display grand totals and subtotals to a pivot table?
- How to sort, filter and group items in a pivot table?

- How to perform calculations?
- How to use slicers to filter a pivot table?
- How to create pivot charts?

After reading this Excel book you will be able to create pivot tables and use all the available tools and functions to perform Excel data analysis easily. You will be able to create various Excel pivot tables from just one data source which summarises the data in different ways. If you have never used pivot tables before then you will learn how easy it is to analyse large data sets without using formulas. You will be able to use pivot tables in Excel dashboards and create slicers to summarise and dissect information in your pivot tables.

You can buy the book from Amazon by entering either of the links below to your web browser:

Amazon US:

www.amazon.com/Excel-Bible-Beginners-Analysis-Crunching/dp/B08BF2V4R4

Amazon UK:

www.amazon.co.uk/Excel-Bible-Beginners-Analysis-Crunching/dp/B08BF2V4R4

Excel Bible for Beginners: Excel for Dummies Guide to the Best Excel Tools, Tips and Shortcuts you Must Know

Excel Bible for Beginners: Excel for Dummies Guide to the Best Excel Tools, Tips and Shortcuts you Must Know includes all the best Excel shortcuts, tools and tips to save you time, increase productivity and help you become more efficient with your worksheets.

Some of the topics this book covers includes:

- How to hide specific text in a worksheet
- How to quickly insert multiple rows using shortcut keys
- How to quickly shift between lots of open Excel windows
- How to repeat your last actions using just one keystroke
- How to get quick access to your favourite command buttons
- How to use the Camera tool
- How to quickly remove duplicate entries using the Advanced Filter tool
- How to quickly split text in one cell into multiple columns

- How to quickly format dates from US to UK format and vice versa
- How to make Excel speak back at you
- How to automatically populate data
- How to change data from column format to row format and vice versa
- How to make your worksheets very hidden
- How to analyse large datasets using Pivot Tables
- How to create two-way lookups
- How to access hidden features that are not available in the ribbon
- How to use some Excel formulas and functions to manipulate data quickly
- And much more!

You can buy the book from Amazon by entering either of the below links to your web browser:

Amazon US:

www.amazon.com/Excel-Bible-Beginners-Dummies-Shortcuts/dp/B08NF32JY6

Amazon UK:

www.amazon.co.uk/Excel-Bible-Beginners-Dummies-Shortcuts/dp/B08NF32JY6

Excel Bible for Beginners: Excel for Dummies Book Containing the Most Awesome Ready to use Excel VBA Macros

If you would like to automate your worksheets and workbooks by using macros then *Excel Bible for Beginners: Excel for Dummies Book Containing the Most Awesome Ready to use Excel VBA Macros* is the book for you. This book will provide you with the best and most useful readymade macros so you can just copy and paste them straight into your workbooks to automate Excel tasks and save you time and effort.

Some of the readymade macros in this book include:

- Unhide all worksheets in the workbook
- Auto fit all columns and rows
- Insert multiple columns and rows in one go
- Create a backup of the current workbook and save it
- Create an email message and attach a workbook to it

- Highlight misspelled words
- Create charts
- Format all charts in a worksheet
- Word count an entire worksheet
- Create a pivot table
- Save a selected range as a PDF
- Create a data entry form
- Create a table of contents
- And much more!

You can buy the book from Amazon by entering either of the below link to your web browser:

Amazon US:

www.amazon.com/Excel-Bible-Beginners-Dummies-Containing/dp/B08T48JCBN

Amazon UK:

www.amazon.co.uk/Excel-Bible-Beginners-Dummies-Containing/dp/B08T48JCBN

Leave a Review
What did you think of this book?

First of all, thank you for purchasing this book. I know you could have picked any number of Excel books to read, but you picked this book and for that I am extremely grateful.

I hope that it has improved your Excel skills and you are now knowledgeable and confident in using XLOOKUP. If so, it would be really great if you could share this book with your friends and family by posting to Facebook and Twitter. It would be nice if you can share your experience of reading this book to your friends and family and what you got out from reading the book.

If you enjoyed this book, I'd like to hear from you and hope that you could take some time to post a review on Amazon. Your feedback and support will help me to greatly improve my writing craft for future projects and make this book even better.

You can leave a book review on Amazon by entering either of the below links to your web browser:

Amazon US:

www.amazon.com/review/create-review?&asin= B08F73L8V5

Amazon UK:

www.amazon.co.uk/review/create-review?&asin= B08F73L8V5

I want you, the reader, to know that your review is very important to me and so, if you'd like to leave a review, all you have to do is enter the above link to your web browser and away you go. I wish you all the best in your future success and happy Excel learning!

Printed in Great Britain
by Amazon